TABLE OF CONTENTS

LIST OF FIGURES

THIS PAGE INTENTIONALLY LEFT BLANK

LIST OF TABLES

.

THIS PAGE INTENTIONALLY LEFT BLANK

LIST OF ACRONYMS AND ABBREVIATIONS

AoR—Area of Responsibility

CBO—Congressional Budget Office

CMR—Civil-Military Relations

COIN—Counterinsurgency

DoD—Department of Defense

DoS—Department of State

MPF—Military Provider Firm

MSDF—Military Security and Defense Firm

MCF—Military Consultant Firm

MIF—Military Intelligence Firm

MLF—Military logistics Firm

MSF—Military Support Firm

OE—Operational Environment

OEF—Operation Enduring Freedom

OIF—Operation Iraqi Freedom

PCMF—Privately Contracted Military Firm

PIB—Public International Body

PMC—Private Military Company

PMI—Private Military Industry

PSC—Private Security Company

RoE—Rules of Engagement

TNC—Trans–National Corporations

USG –United States Government

THIS PAGE INTENTIONALLY LEFT BLANK

I.   INTRODUCTION

Contracts. Outsourcing. Private security. Not so long ago, these terms were more synonymous with corporate business practices than elements of warfare. But times have changed. No longer is the U.S. military alone conducting the myriad of tasks involved within the full spectrum of "modern warfare"—a term which now implies reconstruction and diplomacy in addition to, and often more so than, actual combat. There are three primary reasons for this trend and the author recommends that they be retained throughout this thesis as no serious analytical discussions can occur without their recognition.

First, as Thomas Bruneau states in *Patriots for Profit*, "The federal government has spent twenty years downsizing the civil service…in the belief that privatizing as many government functions as possible would introduce private-sector efficiencies."[1] This proved highly beneficial for the privately contracted military firm which became an almost overnight commodity post–Cold War. Years later, the wars in Iraq and Afghanistan, coupled with the federal job cuts, opened the door to a nearly infinite market.

Second, the military's insistence on its current Counter Insurgency tactics, or COIN, has dictated that U.S. forces place an onus on winning the *hearts and minds* of an indigenous population. This has meant an extraordinary shift in capabilities focusing on the market for much needed humanitarian supplies, construction efforts, and training programs—ranging from advising host-nation civic-administrations to training law enforcement officials nationwide. This "nation-building" mind-set is challenging enough for an organization never intended to adopt it, but even more so when one considers that the all-volunteer military is already strained by unprecedented deployment rotations, training cycles, and an almost unsustainable operational tempo designed to placate both.

---

[1] Thomas C. Bruneau, *Patriots for Profit* (Stanford, CA: Stanford University Press, 2011), 163.

1

Third, there is a strong demand for protection and security measures beyond that which is habitually provided by the U.S. military. For example, in a sensitive geopolitical theater, like Iraq, security can mean everything from guarding VIPs to securing critical facilities. This is especially true when you consider that elements of the U.S. State Department (DoS) and agencies such as the United States Agency for International Development (USAID) often take the lead in the aforementioned markets. Furthermore, these elements have never had any substantial custodial relationship with the U.S. military or the DoD. To do so would imply subordination rather than equality—an occurrence that, rightfully, should be avoided. The government's push to privatize certain facets of the federal market, the nuances of COIN tactics, and the demand for tailored security are separate but linked causal variables in the proliferation of Privately Contracted Military Firms.

The Privately Contracted Military Firm (PCMF)—a relatively new term—is a dynamic and controversial entity. Fluid and adaptable beyond the standard conventions of most corporations, they are not restricted to geographical boundaries and, by design, can take extraordinary measures to navigate around legal restrictions intended to contain them. The PCMF is the focal point of this thesis, but it is part of the larger Private Military Industry (PMI). Interestingly, there is, as of yet, no universally accepted definition of the PMI even though its resources and provisions have permeated throughout the entire process of U.S. military force projection and diplomatic influence. The industry—through various PCMFs—manages all manner of contracted functions within all areas of U.S. national interests. Yet, ironically, it is seldom referred to publicly as a legitimate force multiplier, even though its existence, and subsequent inclusion, within the parameters of modern warfare is universally understood. This presents an interesting paradigm. Outside the specific language of any given contract between a PCMF and the hiring party, there is little understanding of their costs, functions, expectations, and legal boundaries. This is perhaps by design as such ambiguity provides both the desired operational latitude for the *principal* and plausible deniability for the *agent.*[2] This opaque way of doing business carries with it a stench of corruption and erodes public and international trusts in the motives behind the efforts. The U.S., as the standard bearer for emerging democratic societies, needs to set a different course.

Almost every PCMF is viewed with some degree of skepticism by the international and domestic public. This apprehension stems from poor business practices, accusations of over-inflated charges, and tragic consequences garnering global attention and exposing little (if any) substantial legal control measures. Favorable public opinion, however, although coveted by democratic governments, is not the determining factor in continuing business relationships. If it were, then the logical choice would be for the U.S. to distance itself from PCMF utilization and, ultimately, sever its ties to the industry as a whole. But the truth of the matter is that the PMI has become so intertwined in U.S. force projection that severing ties with it is neither reasonable nor altogether prudent. The PMI, after all, provides resources and capabilities that allow the U.S. to conduct global force projection far more efficiently that it could otherwise. Since separating the DoD from the PMI seems altogether untenable, it begs the paramount question: "how can the U.S. remain reliant on the capabilities of the PMI, i.e., continue to award lucrative contracts to PCMFs, without damaging its internationally (and sometimes domestically) delicate reputation"?

This thesis holds that the *quid pro quo* relationship between the U.S. and the PMI *can* and *should* be better defined through legitimate measures of reform. The PNSR[3] has already identified the need for reforms across the entire U.S. national security sector but

---

[2] I am referring here to the principal-agent problem. In political science and economics, the principal-agent problem or agency dilemma treats the difficulties that arise under conditions of incomplete and asymmetric information when a principal hires an agent, such as the problem of potential moral hazard and conflict of interest, in as much as the principal is – presumably – hiring the agent to pursue the principal's interests. The principal-agent problem is found in most employer/employee relationships. Political science has noted the problems inherent in the delegation of legislative authority to bureaucratic agencies. In this case the principal would be the hiring party while the PCMF represents the agent.

[3] The *Project for National Security Reform*, a congressionally funded think tank begun in 2006 with the goal of recommending and implementing, where applicable, institutional reform measures within the U.S. national security system. The director, James R. Locher III, was a prominent figure during the development of the Goldwater–Nichols Defense Reorganization Act of 1986. PNSR's first report, *Forging a New Shield*, was a hefty 830 page document. *See*, also, Thomas C. Bruneau, *Patriots for Profit*, Introduction.

unfortunately, their report has remained largely contained within "the beltway"[4] Although nowhere near as large or detailed, this current project at least hopes to have a distant relation—even if only in intent—to the ambitions of the PNSR. The recommendations advanced herein would set the conditions for PCMFs to become much more accountable for their actions universally, i.e., to the hiring principal, the state of origin, and to the state within which the PCMF would conduct its operations. Further, the recommendations should go a long way toward fostering a better understanding of their capabilities and limitations. This would, and more importantly, should, facilitate the inclusion of PCMFs and their parent PMI into the published national security strategies of the United States. This move would not be without controversy, but it is altogether fitting that the U.S. take this major step forward. It is a measure that is past due. Whatever opinions of them may be, PCMFs are a twenty-first century reality and should not be met with twentieth century protocol. Furthermore, by including them in the national strategies, the U.S. will have, potentially, introduced the PCMFs as possible third-party actors, thereby fostering greater transparency and democratic control over their utilization. The implications of the former would foster better domestic opinions of an open government while the latter should take measurable steps to strengthen international relations through an open foreign policy.

This thesis advances the hypothesis that establishing a status–based legal framework[5] will promote legitimacy, increase effectiveness, and mitigate concerns—both domestically and abroad. This will be accomplished through six chapters. Chapter I has already introduced a relatively new term into the field's lexicon—the Privately Contracted Military Firm (PCMF)—a term that should be retained as a necessary tool in defining further PCMF sub-classifications and, ultimately, advance this thesis' endeavors. Next, Chapter II will examine the origin(s) and evolution of PCMFs as well as classify them into six separate entities. Chapter III will look to the Vietnam War and the relationships and decisions within certain political circles that this author suggests set

---

[4] Washington, DC.

[5] I am referring here to legal parameters designed to effectively monitor and influence PCMF behavior. This transcends the expectations defined (if at all) within the contractual agreement by codifying international legal norms. The framework would be an institutionalized process but adaptable enough to be applicable to any of the six PCMF classifications defined Chapter II.

precedents cementing future U.S. reliance on PCMFs. Chapter IV addresses PCMF utilization in modern warfare—specifically within the Iraqi theater of operations—as a likely trend so intrinsic to U.S. force projection that it requires amending the way the U.S. military conducts business. Chapter V builds upon the latter and addresses the peculiar lack of official recognition of PCMFs by the U.S. throughout its published network of security strategies and the effects these omissions may be having on U.S. civil–military relations. Chapter VI presents the current legal measures in place that hold PCMFs accountable, describe the weaknesses within these measures, and examines the institutions and legal reforms necessary to achieve a feasible resolution.

THIS PAGE INTENTIONALLY LEFT BLANK

II. THE EVOLUTION OF WARFARE—HOW DID WE GET HERE?

> *The members of the [private military security] firm were polite and generally helpful, but the ambiguity between who they were and what they were doing always hung in the air. They were employees of a private company, but were performing tasks inherently military. It just did not settle with the way [Americans] tended to understand either business or warfare. However, there they were, simply doing their jobs, but in the process, altering the entire security balance of the region.[6]*

The emergence of PCMFs as U.S. force multipliers is nothing new, but their level of integration into current American military operations borders on the alarming. This chapter will take a look at this relationship in two distinct parts. Part one is dedicated to history of the PCMF and discusses reasons why the U.S. has come to utilize PCMFs so extensively. Part two defines the PCMF and classifies its sub-sets into six separate functions, offering insight into each one's respective capabilities and provisions. When taken together, these two parts will lay the groundwork for the reform measures I believe necessary for proper legal oversight and control.

A. ORIGINS AND RISE OF THE PRIVATELY CONTRACTED MILITARY FIRM (PCMF)

The U.S. military has a long history of utilizing civilian support during military operations. Even during the Revolutionary War, General George Washington's Continental Army relied on civilians for transportation, carpentry, engineering, food, and medical services. The benefits of such an arrangement were immediately recognizable. By utilizing civilians to perform such services, soldiers were able to focus on their core task of war fighting.[7] The relationship was mutually beneficial as the civilians performed functions that, according to Steven Zamparelli were either "too menial for soldiers or

---

[6] P.W. Singer, *Corporate Warriors: The Rise of the Privatized Military Industry*, 3rd ed. (Ithaca, NY: Cornell University Press, 2008), vii. This quote describes members of the PCMF – MPRI during Singer's encounter with them in the Balkans, circa 1996.

[7] William W. Epley, "Civilian Support of Field Armies," *Army Logistician* 22 (November/December 1990): 1–6.

were [already] well-established or specialized in commercial industry."[8] Contracting out services grew in scope over both World Wars and Korea, and by the time America had entered Vietnam it had become an accepted practice. Although not a common occurrence, soldiers had grown accustomed to seeing U.S. civilians on the battlefield and this held true until about twenty years ago, as the ratio between civilian contractors and soldiers remained relatively constant (see Table 1). The end of the Cold War, however, signaled a change, shifting formerly random encounters between soldiers and civilians into an everyday, everyplace occurrence.

The end of the Cold War brought substantial changes to the way the U.S. projected its forces into areas of geo-political interest. The dissolution of the former Soviet Union created a market for customizable security forces, consulting services, and logistical/support firms almost overnight. The U.S. military for obvious reasons could not provide these measures in any substantial fashion, yet still had the desire to protect U.S. interests in Western Europe. PCMFs were quick to capitalize on the European security vacuum and found a willing financier in an eager American government.

If Post-Cold War provided the initial push for PCMF growth, then the aftermath of 9/11 could be credited with providing a substantial surge. The satellites of the former Soviet Union were of course of U.S. strategic interests but the events of 9/11 brought us into war. For the first time in a decade we had a declared enemy—Al Qaeda—and the need to rapidly establish a decisive military presence on foreign soil—Afghanistan. The war in Afghanistan would strengthen U.S. reliance on PCMFs. As the U.S. turned its eye towards Iraq, this relationship would be solidified.

---

[8] Steven J. Zamparelli, "Competitive Sourcing and Privatization: Contractors on the Battlefield: What Have We Signed Up For?" *Air Force Journal of Logistics* (Fall, 1999): 14, taken from Stephen M. Blizzard's article "Increasing Reliance on Contractors on the Battlefield; How Do We Keep from Crossing the Line?" *Air Force Journal of Logistics* 23 no. 3 (1999): 7.

Table 1.   Presence of contractor support during U.S. military operations (After Bruneau, 2011)

Conflict	Estimated in thousands		Estimated ratio of contractor to military personnel*
	Contractor*	Military	
Revolutionary War	2	9	1 to 6
War of 1812	n.a.	38	n.a.
Mexican-American War	6	33	1 to 6
Civil War	200	1,000	1 to 5
Spanish-American War	n.a.	35	n.a.
World War I	85	2,000	1 to 24
World War II	734	5,400	1 to 7
Korea	156	393	1 to 2.5
Vietnam	70	359	1 to 5
Gulf War	9**	500	1 to 55**
Balkans	20	20	1 to 1
Iraq Theater as of 2010***	150	150	1 to 1

SOURCE: Congressional Budget Office based on data from William W. Epley, "Civilian Support of Field Armies," *Army Logistician*, vol. 22 (November/December 1990), pp. 30-35; Steven J. Zamparelli, "Contractors on the Battlefield: What Have We Signed Up For?" *Air Force Journal of Logistics*, vol. 23, no. 3 (Fall 1999), pp. 10-19; Department of Defense, *Report on DoD Program for Planning, Managing, and Accounting for Contractor Services and Contractor Personnel During Contingency Operations* (October 2007), p. 12; Thomas C. Bruneau, *Patriots for Profit*, (Stanford, CA: Stanford University Press, 2011), 115. Data in the Public Domain.

NOTE: n.a. = not available

*For some conflicts, the estimated number of contractor personnel includes civilians employed by the U.S. government. However, because most civilians present during military operations are contractor personnel, the inclusion of government civilians should not significantly affect the calculated ratio of contractor personnel to military personnel.

**The government of Saudi Arabia provided significant amounts of products and services during Operations Desert Shield and Desert Storm. Personnel associated with those provisions are not included in the data or the ratio.

***For this study, the Congressional Budget Office considers the following countries to be part of the Iraq Theater: Iraq, Bahrain, Jordan, Kuwait, Oman, Qatar, Saudi Arabia, Turkey, and the United Arab Emirates.[9]

---

[9] The notes from Table 1.1 are taken exclusively from Thomas C. Bruneau, *Patriots for Profit* (Stanford CA: Stanford University Press, 2011), 115, updated through open source.

Despite the swift expansion in PCMF growth post-Cold War, up until 2001, PCMFs had largely gone unnoticed by the general public, having functioned in areas of both geographical and operational disinterest. Their size and scope were comparatively small to that of the military, and most of their operations had focused on VIP security measures or serving in advisory positions. But the United States' declaration of a "global war on terror" and, subsequently, the invasions of Afghanistan and Iraq would expand both their roles and their demands. The United States and its allies would rapidly need to mobilize specialized security forces with tremendous operational latitude. PCMFs seized the chance to fill this need and, a decade later, they are still evolving.

Although contractors, as a whole, have been tied to military force projection throughout history, the rise of the Privately Contracted Military Firm (PCMF) and, subsequently, the degree to which they now serve as force multipliers and, in some instances, almost entirely independent options, is unprecedented. In fact, since 2003, the ratio of contractors to soldiers on the battlefield—specifically, in Iraq—has evolved such that now it has swung in favor of the contractors. This statistic was made dramatically clear during the U.S. withdrawal in 2011, wherein contractors outnumbered U.S. servicemen and women by 2–1. These figures are sobering from a financial point of view, as the economic effect of employing contractors is significant. But perhaps of even greater significance is the political controversy surrounding the utilization of civilian contractors in pursuit of U.S. strategic objectives on foreign soil. Such a course of action has inherently delicate political concerns, as the court of international public opinion has rarely viewed hired civilian security entities in a positive light. Over the past several years U.S. Administrations have omitted the mention of PCMFs (at least directly) as force providers within any of the nation's three security strategy documents—a move designed to placate international concerns over their use. But the omission is strikingly peculiar, as the utilization of PCMFs is a very real and seemingly necessary occurrence during times of conflict. In fact, PCMFs are now so intrinsically tied to modern U.S. force projection that the Quadrennial Defense Review (QDR) mentions their costs and contributions despite omission by the respective strategic documents. The author recognizes that Administrations rightfully seek to craft documents that provide them with political latitude and, where necessary, plausible deniability. But excluding PCMFs from the security strategies is ignoring the elephant in the living room and, in actuality, providing the companies themselves with enough leeway to operate outside of traditional legal measures and largely absent from public view, subsequently providing contracted personnel, provisions, and resources at a potentially higher cost—both financially and politically.

Since 2001, the world has changed dramatically. Although the private military industry (PMI) as a whole has been intrinsically linked to U.S. force projection, its influence on American executive political decisions was largely unknown—or, at least not publicly accepted. During Vietnam for example, companies such as Brown & Root held significant positions of influence due to their enhanced logistical support capabilities, but this influence remained largely contained within high–level, political circles. The end of the Cold War also contributed significantly to the rise of the PMI— in fact, some scholarly works point to the Cold War's demise as the *dominating* factor for PMI proliferation. Although this thesis agrees with the latter conclusion, it points out that there was little domestic recognition, outside confined, senior-ranking, political circles, over PMI proliferation. Post–2001, however, ushered in unprecedented public awareness that U.S. reliance on logistical/support companies like Brown & Root was not only an almost unavoidable necessity, but also a means of profit for similar privatized companies.[10] Furthermore, the U.S. needed rapid security capabilities seemingly beyond the reach of the U.S. armed forces. Companies such as the former Blackwater quickly filled the void and expanded the scope and responsibilities of privatized security far beyond what it had previously been. The two examples listed above are indicative of how the U.S. operates across the entire spectrum of modern warfare. From combat missions, to contingency operations, to humanitarian relief and reconstruction operations, the U.S. is continuing to outsource its requirements at an alarming rate.

---

[10] The events of 9/11 triggered the invasion into Afghanistan and had significant influence over the decision to invade Iraq. The DoD needed both large–scale logistical support and tactical security enhancement with rapid deployment capabilities beyond those of the U.S. military at the time. Coupled with the attractiveness of keeping military personnel numbers low, PCMFs became a valuable commodity. The confluence of events post–9/11 altered, perhaps forever, U.S. modern warfare.

As the leader of the free world, the United States is looked upon as a trend setter for democratic progress. Consequently, the United States' extensive use of PCMFs has caused others to seek similar recourses and facilitated continued acceptance of PCMFs as a ready and relevant option for security-force enhancement. Ironically, the precedents set by the United States' commitment to PCMF utilization may actually be changing how U.S. force projection is perceived and/or accepted internationally. The growing demands for immediate security, with minimal public scrutiny, coupled with the actions of the U.S. have caused PCMFs to grow swiftly. But this rapid expansion of force options has generated divisive debates, often testing the boundaries of civil-military relations and redefining a states' "monopoly of force."

Utilization of PCMFs may allow a nation or organization to buy or supplement its own security for an indeterminate period of time. This provides the consumer with significant political latitude and a certain degree of separation, i.e., PCMFs offer plausible deniability of active, uniformed service involvement while still providing para-military forces capable of preserving states' self-interests. But sometimes the purchase of this commodity can have horrific consequences, actually causing strategy to drive policy—a situation that, according to Clausewitz, is to be avoided at all costs,[11] e.g., Blackwater, Worldwide, Inc., Nisour Square, Baghdad, 2007.[12]

The possibilities of backlash have not deterred growth, however, and PCMFs have found an unmistakable niche in modern times. So much so that personnel assigned to PCMFs now outnumber military personnel in Iraq two to one.[13] Such figures are generating significant questions. Has the proliferation of PCMFs grown so large that they are now part of the decision cycle in planning the U.S. armed forces' structure, role, and involvement in future conflicts? If so, why are they not officially recognized by U.S.

---

[11] Carl von Clausewitz, *On War,* edited and translated by Michael Howard and Peter Paret (Princeton, NJ: Princeton University Press, 1984), *passim.*

[12] Jeremy Scahill, *Blackwater, The Rise of the World's Most Powerful Mercenary Army* (New York: Nation Books, 2007).

[13] Special Inspector General, Iraq Reconstruction (SIGIR), *Quarterly Report to the United States Congress,* SIGIR, July 2011.

administrations?[14] How are the decisions to utilize PCMFs (and their subsequent actions) affecting U.S. foreign relations? Should the international arena recognize PCMFs as third-party actors (after nation-states and militaries)? And, what are the consequences if they do?[15]

The recognition of PCMF relevance raises some significant concerns. Critics argue that by utilizing PCMFs, America is simply employing mercenaries operating outside the law, and, therefore, that the risks of PCMF employment are not acceptable— politically and economically. Conversely, proponents might concede that the existence of PCMFs prevents a monopoly of force—a threat to democracy professed by the Founding Fathers[16] and summarized by Samuel Huntington's book *The Soldier and the State*.[17] PCMFs would, therefore, not only be necessary in the ideology of the former, but beneficial in the missive of the latter, as an entity existing outside direct political influence while operating with military-like professionalism.

B. CLASSIFYING THE PCMF

Perhaps one of the biggest hurdles in achieving any substantial reform revolves around the tremendous amount of confusion involving the naming conventions within the private military industry. Lack of any significantly definitive classification has made enforcing any tangible legal control measures almost impossible as the expected behavior and/or provisions of the respective contracted entity are ambiguous at best. Classification, therefore, does more than accurately name the company and actually implies a pre-meditated course of action and makes enforcing accountability much more

---

[14] The U.S. has recognized the importance of PCMFs within the QDR but this is post-facto. Oddly, there is no mention, at least directly, of PCMFs within any of the United States' official security documents: the National Security Strategy (NSS) issued from the President, the National Defense Strategy (NDS) – issued from the Secretary of Defense, or the National Military Strategy (NMS) – issued from the Chairman of the Joint Chiefs of Staff.

[15] The 2006 Quadrennial Review, (QDR) recognizes Private Military Companies and the impacts that their tactical and operational effects are having in the strategic realm.

[16] Michael I. Meyerson, *Liberty's Blueprint: How Madison and Hamilton Wrote the Federalist Papers, Defined the Constitution, and Made Democracy Safe for the World* (New York: Basic Books, 2008).

[17] Samuel P. Huntington, *The Soldier and the State: The Theory and Politics of Civil–Military Relations* (Cambridge, MA: Belknap Press, 1981, first ed. published 1957). In this instance I am referring to Sam Huntington's theory of "professionalizing" the military's officer corps as a means to ensure objective civilian control through indirect means.

feasible. Drawing heavily from Peter Singer and Huma T. Yasin,[18] this section will define the privately contracted military firm and its sub-classifications.

Originally, most scholarly works and those within certain political/business circles referred to the "private military firm," or "private military company" but this implied an offensive characteristic. Trying to distance themselves from this military-centric classification, the companies began to refer to themselves as "private *security* companies." Most recently, these two terms have been combined to form the name: "private military security companies." Although these terms are still much in use today throughout most scholarly works, this thesis argues that the term privately contracted military firm, or PCMF, best encompasses the interested point of study. This proposal is accurately supported by Huma Yasin who "refers to the industry as 'privately contracted military firms' to highlight the three essential, defining characteristics of the PCMF: the organizations are (1) privately held corporations; (2) employed under a contractual arrangement; (3) performing traditional military duties."[19]

Further complicating the previously held methods of classifying PCMFs was the suggested implementation of "terms such as 'active' and 'passive' and 'armed' and 'unarmed' but these labels ignore the vast differences between PCMFs in scope and objective."[20] Peter Singer, one of the leading experts in PCMF operations, suggests that the PCMFs are so broad in their provisions, often blending economic and military fundamentals, that the industry should be further broken down (and classified) based on the range of the services they can provide.[21] Singer identifies three broad categories of PCMFs but Yasin takes this provision further and advances six separate categories—each of which this thesis concludes is wholly applicable to its own endeavors and so, includes them here:

---

[18] P. W. Singer, cited in Huma Yasin, *Playing Catchup: Proposing the Creation of Status-Based Regulations to Bring Private Military Contractor Firms Within the Purview of International and Domestic Law*. Professionl Report written as a LL.M. Candidate, Southern Methodist University School of Law. 2012.

[19] Yasin, *Playing Catchup*, 445.

[20] Ibid., 446.

[21] Ibid.

Ordering firms from those performing functions most similar to a traditional military to the least, the classification is as follows: (1) Military Provider Firms; (2) Military Security or Defense Firms; (3) Military Intelligence Firms; (4) Military Consultant Firms; (5) Military Logistic Firms; and (6) Military Support Firms.[22]

1. Military Provider Firms

Military Provider Firms (MPFs) are the tactical force providers to the purchasing agent. MPFs can operate distinctly on their own as a tactical combat force or can augment the capabilities of forces already on the ground. Additionally, MPFs can provide a tremendous amount of specialized resources, capable of being tailored to the missions' demands. This means that their services are highly desirable to even well-developed countries with significant military forces. Perhaps the most notable MPF is the firm, Executive Outcomes (EO). EO was founded in 1989 and is part of the Strategic Resources Corporation—a larger South African venture-capital firm. EO is unique in two primary areas. First, EO recruited almost exclusively from the standing South African Defence Force. This provided a significant tactical advantage as recruits would arrive to EO with a similar foundation of tactics, techniques, and procedures and could thereby be seamlessly integrated into a cohesive fighting force. In fact, EO was such a viable, ready-made combat force provider that, as Yasin observes, "[they] served as a total force provider in Sierra Leone in 1991." Second, EO operated under the corporate umbrella of a larger firm with myriad regional interests. This was a symbiotic relationship, providing EO with substantial cover to elicit contracts beyond the reach of what should be expected from an MPF, while providing its parent organization a physical presence within areas of geopolitical interest.

2. Military Security and Defense Firms

Military Security and Defense Firms (MSDFs) may be the most highly publicized form of a PCMF and, in most instances, account for the tremendous amount of public concern regarding their actions. Often referred to as Private Security Companies (PSCs),

---

22 Yasin, *Playing Catch–Up*, 446.

15

MSDFs are, primarily, defensive in nature but they have become so intertwined in U.S. force protection measures that they are sometimes difficult to distinguish from the armed forces. Legal classification and regulations are perhaps the most ambiguous with this PCMF, and thus, the MSDF has garnered the lion's share of scrutiny—perhaps none more so than the MSDF, Blackwater.[23] Blackwater is a private corporation which began in 1998 in North Carolina. Through a series of personal contacts, Blackwater's founder, Eric Prince was able to generate substantial (and often, unprecedented) contracts at all levels—state, federal, and even international. "In February, 2000, Blackwater won a General Services Administration (GSA) contract, which facilitated the U.S. government purchasing products or services from Blackwater without having to evaluate and accept bids on the competitive market."[24] Since 2001, this lucrative relationship has empowered Blackwater to expand exponentially in scope and influence, equating to a staggering growth rate of 80,453%.[25]

3. Military Intelligence Firms

Military Intelligence Firms (MIFs)[26] provide the historically state-based function of intelligence procurement and analysis. The emergence of the MIF is contentious at best, as the sensitive level of their services can easily trespass into a sovereign state's domain. But nonetheless, MIFs have emerged as a valuable commodity in areas of conflict and/or instability. For example, during OEF and OIF, it swiftly became apparent that the U.S. intelligence structure would need substantial reforms and/or assistance to

---

[23] For the purpose of continuity this company will be referred to throughout this thesis as *Blackwater*. It should be noted, however, that Blackwater has changed its name twice since 2007, first, to *Xe* and second (and currently), to *Academi*. Popular speculation is that Blakwater did this to escape the stigma surrounding the company's actions in Iraq in 2007. *See, Blackwater and Nisour Square.*

[24] Yasin, *Playing Catchup*, 452

[25] Ibid.

[26] Yasin highlights that this category has not been distinguished from the other PCMFs by contemporary scholarship, as the procurement of intelligence has previously been considered the primary domain of states. *See* Walter Pincus, *Increase in Contracting Intelligence Jobs Raising Concerns*, Washington Post, March 20, 2006. Additionally, the sensitive nature of obtaining intelligence from individuals increases the potential to commit violations of human rights. *See War Profiteer of the Month: CACI*, 23 War Profiteers' News (April, 14, 2010), http://www.wri-irg.org/node/9927 (discussing the accountability of interrogators working for CACI as regards torturing detainees). For the purpose of this thesis, however, MIFs will be a separate and thus, identifiable category of a PCMF.

operate effectively in the COIN environment. MIFs helped fill the intelligence gap. CACI is just such a MIF. CACI was formed in 1962, initially offering simulation software to its clients. Like most PCMFs, CACI took advantage of the end of the Cold War and offered information technology to the federal government. By 1998, CACI began acquiring several smaller intelligence firms, thus "becoming a premier provider of information technology services."[27] "In 2006, CACI was one of seven contractors chosen by the U.S. Army to provide technology and engineering services worth as much as $19 billion over a ten-year period."[28] This contract is alarming considering CACI's involvement in the Abu Ghraib scandal[29]—perhaps indicative of the reliance on their rather unique skill provisions.

4. Military Consultant Firms

Military Consultant Firms (MCFs) serve in, primarily, advisory roles without any direct involvement in combat operations alongside their client. The distinguishing characteristic of MCFs from other PCMFs is that they are not physically present on the battlefield. This, however, does not imply that their value is any less than those of other PCMFs. On the contrary, MCFs are often considered the brain trust of the Private Military Industry and as such have an extensive amount of influence. Military Professional Resources Incorporation (MPRI) is a prominent MCF. Founded in 1978, MPRI has a proven track record as a partner of U.S. military endeavors. MPRI has extensive ties to the highest levels of the U.S. government with over ninety-five percent of its employee pool having served in the U.S. Army. "MPRI became invaluable in the mid-1990s for its strategic expertise in warfare in the former conflict-ridden Yugoslavia."[30] Owing, in large part to their success in Croatia, MPRI won a substantial contract with Bosnia regarding "combat training," but the structure of the contract was

---

[27] Yasin, *Playing Catchup*, 455.

[28] Ibid.

[29] The prisoner abuse scandal of Abu Ghraib, however damaging to the reputation of the United States also had reverberating effects throughout the privatized community. CACI employees were directly linked to the scandal and, to some degree, were even considered to be acting in supervisory roles. The significance of such a statement cannot be understated as it meant that civilians were in direct control over military personnel during combat related operations.

[30] Yasin, *Playing Catchup*, 458

somewhat of an anomaly—the Bosnian government received the military training but Saudi Arabia, Malaysia, Kuwait, Brunei, and the United Arab Emirates funded the payment.[31] Currently, MPRI is heavily invested as a training/advisory force in Iraq and Afghanistan.[32]

5.   Military Logistics Firms

Military Logistics Firms (MLFs) provide support unrelated to direct combat operations, such as transportation, mail delivery, cargo handling, and refueling. Ironically, while they serve in a supporting role, MLFs often travel into hostile areas to do so. The largest provider of such functions is the MLF, Kellogg, Brown & Root (KBR). Founded in 1919, this Texas-based firm has risen to prominence as the single, largest PCMF in American history.[33] "In 1963, Halliburton, a global construction and energy services company, purchased KBR as a subsidiary corporation…[but] officially separated from KBR forty-four years later, in April of 2007."[34] Like Blackwater, KBR has been a center for controversy and scrutiny, but for a much longer time. Over the past fifty years, KBR has had dubious relationships with senior U.S. government officials, ranging from President Lyndon B. Johnson to Vice President Dick Cheney.

It is not too farfetched to conclude that KBR ran the U.S. operations in Iraq—at least logistically. As Yasin succinctly states:

> Between 2003 and the summer of 2007, KBR had solidified over $20 billion in logistics and support contracts—a number roughly *three times* what the U.S. government paid to fight the *entire* 1991 Persian Gulf

---

[31] Ibid., 460. This setup reveals a very important issue with regard to PCMFs that the law has not fully addressed—the extent to which states can fund private militaries to perform tactical or combat operations that serve the funding states' interests.

[32] The author has worked extensively with MPRI contractors in Iraq and has observed the evolution of a provincial-wide law enforcement training program designed to instruct Iraqi National Police how to conduct forensics and crime scene investigations in accordance with proven methods of accuracy. The program known as Combined Law Enforcement Against Terrorism (CLEAT) was initiated by MPRI contractors in 2009 with measurable degrees of success, first in Ramadi and Fallujah, then throughout the entire Anbar Province.

[33] So much so that this thesis will address KBR, how it rose to prominence, and the causal effects their emergence had on the PMI as a whole, in Chapter II.

[34] Yasin, *Playing Catchup*, 461.

War. On March 2, 2010, the government awarded another comprehensive logistics contract to KBR."[35]

6. Military Support Firms

Military Support Firms (MSFs) are, by far, the largest of the six categories of PCMFs. MSFs provide all the necessary, and usually large-scale, operations required to house significant numbers of U.S. military personnel. Basic essential provisions like food services, laundry operations, construction/maintenance projects, and power generation are all the hallmark of MSFs. KBR, again, is the prominent player here and is the largest support firm in Iraq.[36]

The majority of scholarly works categorize MLFs and MSFs together,[37] but this thesis seconds the recommendation of Huma Yasin—that separating the two is essential for effective legal reform. This section contends this to be a reasonable objective since, unlike MLFs, MSFs reside and operate within the confines and security of military bases and therefore should not be subject to the same legal parameters.

Conclusion

Although the history of the modern day PCMF is certainly significant to this thesis, the primary focus of the chapter was on PCMF classification. Misidentifying PCMFs, or worse, applying blanket legalese to the entire industry not only fails to prevent fraud and abuse, it may actually encourage it. Without being able to succinctly determine which type of PCMF is performing what and for whom, current legal measures are simply irrelevant, making any realistic hopes of achieving PCMF accountability nearly impossible. For this purpose, this chapter presented six sub-classifications to be retained for further debate during the advancement of the author's hypothesis.

---

[35] Yasin, *Playing Catch Up*, 462. *See*, also Singer, *Corporate Warriors*, 247.

[36] Yasin, *Playing Catchup*, 463.

[37] I am thinking here of P.W. Singer, Dan Briody, Deborah Avant, *et al.*

THIS PAGE INTENTIONALLY LEFT BLANK

III.   PRESIDENTS, MOTIVES, AND PROFITS: HOW THE MODERN-DAY PCMF MAY HAVE BEEN BORN IN VIETNAM

As we have seen in Chapter I, the use of private military institutions is nothing new. Throughout the history of warfare kings, presidents, and prime ministers have found ways to employ at their respective discretions units of enforcers, guardians, and suppliers whose existence remained outside the scope of traditional military means. This privatization of war has given the executive immense political latitude by providing him with a means to exercise force, provide additional support, or project influence into areas that otherwise may have been (at least politically) untenable. Although this chapter builds on Chapter I—that the end of the Cold War contributed greatly to the rapid expansion of PCMFs—it proposes that the precedents set years earlier may have had greater significant impact than most modern PCMF related works recognize.

Part one of this chapter will look to the Vietnam War, specifically, and present evidence that the issues, relationships, and decisions that accompanied it could accurately be considered the birthplace of the modern-day PCMF. Part two presents two separate theoretical proposals. First, that the "credibility gap" associated with President Johnson has re-emerged in modern times. And second, that counterinsurgency, or COIN, (like PCMFs) began in earnest in Vietnam and that the same tactics that began there have been reapplied in the Middle East. This not only sets the transition for Chapter III but also implies that the U.S. emphasis on COIN has exacerbated the proliferation of PCMFs.

A.   THE VIETNAM WAR—AN ATYPICAL CONFLICT

The Vietnam War presented the United States with numerous political and military hurdles. The conflict created immense emotional debate during and after the war. But the political decisions—especially the decisions to utilize Private Military Companies in direct, supporting roles—were perhaps of even greater debate, as the decisions by presidents Kennedy, Johnson, and Nixon, respectively, would be instrumental in determining the amount of influence that private military companies (PCMFs) would have on every future application of U.S. force projection. For this reason, this thesis will utilize the Vietnam War as a case study in order to determine the reasons that the aforementioned executives chose to utilize private military companies as combat multipliers across a very diverse spectrum.

This chapter will begin with the assumption that, as a whole, the decision to employ contractors on the battlefield was necessary to solve the critical military problem of Vietnam—fighting an asymmetrical enemy operating in harsh geography. U.S. forces would need to re-evaluate the enemy, the environment, and their own methods to achieve success. This dilemma was succinctly described by Stephen Rosen when he stated that U.S. senior military leaders knew they needed to know "how to adapt, quickly and successfully, to the peculiar and unfamiliar battlefield conditions in which our armed forces [were] fighting."[38] The research question is to determine not only *why* PCMFs were utilized during Vietnam, but *how* they became such an integral entity of sustained combat operations. The relationship between civilian contractors and military operations may have risen from the personal relationships between the respective presidents (most notably Johnson) and senior civilian CEOs. It is a difficult task, however, to form a clear causal link between positions of influence and lucrative investments. As George Herring noted, possibly the "limited vision of the political and military leaders of the time"[39] made them incapable of adjusting to an adaptable enemy (the key component of Rosen's argument), and so, they employed PCMFs out of desperation in order to provide maximum mobility to the military forces. Another interpretive challenge is that effectively determining any quid pro quo between PCMFs and a Commander-in-Chief is speculative at best, as any substantial evidence to the contrary is, at first glance, ambiguous.

This section presents four contributing factors that serve as causes for the utilization of PCMFs on an unprecedented level in Vietnam. In chronological order, these factors (with the applicable Presidents listed in parentheses) are as follows: 1.) The Consistency Theory obligated the United States to perhaps unnecessary involvement in

---

[38] Stephen Peter Rosen, "Vietnam and the American Theory of Limited War," *International Security* 7 (Fall 1982): 83.

[39] George C. Herring, "Johnson Administration's Limited War in Vietnam," *Looking Back on the Vietnam War: A 1990's Perspective on the Decisions, Combat, and Legacies*, eds. William Head and Lawrence E. Grinder (Westport, CT, Greenwood Press, 1993), 90.

Vietnam due to personal sentiments and professional courtesies (Eisenhower, Kennedy, and Johnson), 2.) Unethical professional relationships strongly influenced presidential decisions (Johnson), 3.) An unprepared Congress displayed little proficiency in understanding, much less supervising, hastily contracted expenditures (Johnson), and 4.) Often-damning public opinion, questioning the validity of U.S. involvement in Vietnam, created an environment that was extremely open to exploitation (Johnson and Nixon).

B.   FOUR CAUSAL FACTORS AND THE PRECEDENTS THEY SET

The Vietnam War ushered in a relatively new way of doing business. Prior to this war, U.S. reliance on civilian support had been in a manner that kept the armed services active while keeping the providers largely out of harm's way—at least directly. Contractors still performed the tasks necessary to support standing armies, but they did so in rear areas, mostly free from any direct enemy threat.[40] In Vietnam, however, this tactic began to change. In this conflict, more than any other time in U.S. history, soldiers and contractors worked side by side and shared the inherent dangers of active combat operations. So prevalent was this relationship that *Business Week* referred to Vietnam as a "war by contract."[41]

As Robert Komer points out in *Bureaucracy at War*, "Vietnam presented a highly atypical conflict environment."[42] There were numerous cultural differences and socio-political agendas, as well as military objectives, that were either wholly misunderstood or missed altogether. It had the potential to become a quagmire and in retrospect has been labeled such. But, just as it was an "atypical conflict environment," it offered (from a purely contractual point of view) a unique perspective into the emergence and subsequent integration of PCMFs on the battlefield. Considering what was pushing U.S. policy makers into this quagmire, the first causal factor is *The Consistency Theory*.

---

[40] Zamparelli, "Competitive Sourcing," 14.

[41] "Vietnam: How Business Fights the War on Contract," *Business Week* (5 March, 1965): 58–62.

[42] Robert W. Komer, *Bureaucracy at War, U.S. Performance in the Vietnam Conflict* (Boulder, CO. Westview Press, 1986), 2.

1.   The Consistency Theory

The consistency theory, in essence, suggests that each president was more than likely to continue with the programs, policies, and initiatives begun by his predecessor. This seems a logical assumption, because, at that time, stemming the expansion of communism was a high priority within the government of the United States. President Eisenhower was adamant in his belief that if the U.S. failed to prevent communism from developing in politically fragile nation-states, it would have a domino effect on neighboring countries and/or those in similar conditions of political instability. This strategic concept rendered U.S. military involvement an almost foregone conclusion. The "domino theory articulated by President Eisenhower in 1954 set forth a worst-case scenario and guided strategic thinking thereafter,"[43] Gary Hess observes. Eisenhower, like Truman before him, felt that Vietnam was a target of Soviet and Chinese aggression and therefore (in keeping with the domino theory) was of immense, strategic importance to the U.S.[44] As such, Eisenhower expanded the Military Assistance Advisory Group (MAAG) initially begun by Truman and sent to Vietnam in 1954.[45]

Post WWII and fresh out of the Korean War, the United States held deep concerns regarding communist aggression. But preventing the spread of communism meant positioning U.S. resources in global defense postures. This course of action was a policy of containment and the consequences of such a policy were not lost on those within the Executive Branch. The political intricacies of investing U.S. forces in far-reaching countries, compounded with the deeply held anti-communist sentiments, facilitate an understanding of why successive presidents chose, in large part, to continue the course of their respective predecessors.

---

[43] Gary R. Hess, "South Vietnam Under Siege, 1961-1965: Kennedy, Johnson, and the Question of Escalation or Disengagement," in David L. Anderson, ed., *The Columbia History of the Vietnam War* (New York: Columbia University Press, 2011), 146.

[44] David Anderson, *Trapped by Success, The Eisenhower Administration and Vietnam*, 1953-1961 (New York, Columbia University Press, 1991), 18.

[45] History of the MAAG, accessed through Richmond University, https://facultystaff.richmond.edu/~ebolt/history398/MAAG.html. The MAAG, although comprised of military personnel would advise and assist in training the Vietnamese forces. The MAAG precedent would set the conditions for the rise of the PCMF, the Military Consultant Firm (MCF), *See*, MPRI, Chapter I.

Eisenhower pursued Truman's goal, recognized at the end of the French Indochina War in 1954—the preservation of an independent, pro-Western government in South Vietnam. This government would be an alternative to the communist model and would serve as a sentinel in the region, steadfast against communist aggression. Such a regime would divide the country, but this outcome was a plausible option for the Eisenhower administration as similar precedents had already been set in West Germany and South Korea. "The Eisenhower years saw the development of a large and multi-faceted advisory role. Several U.S. government agencies became involved, including defense and state departments, and private international agencies engaged in humanitarian assistance."[46] But Eisenhower's methods were slow and methodical and offered few tangible examples of success. In fact, the Eisenhower administration seemed to drag its political feet in Vietnam, perhaps in hope that the issue would reach better resolution and thus, provide more viable options under the coming presidential watch of John F. Kennedy. Or maybe Eisenhower never fully grasped the situation in Vietnam and so chose the politically safest course of action—to invest the bare minimum of U.S. support. Regardless of whether Eisenhower purposefully postponed decisions on Vietnam or if he was simply politically ignorant to the area's regional turbulence, the onus of the problem was going to fall on Kennedy's presidency. The irony of Eisenhower's lack of any substantial actions and/or decisions compounded with his administrations' self-proclaimed success would make this responsibility even more daunting. David Anderson states this succinctly in the following:

By 1961 the goal of buying time had been achieved. The Saigon regime had stood for over six years, but South Vietnam was not a viable nation and was not becoming one. The objective of an independent South Vietnam was proving increasingly unrealistic and unachievable without greater cost and risk to the United States. With its proclivity to perceive and proclaim success where, in fact, failure abounded, the Eisenhower administration trapped itself and its successors into a commitment to the survival of its own counterfeit creation.[47]

---

[46] *See*, History of the MAAG, https://facultystaff.richmond.edu/~ebolt/history398/MAAG.html.

[47] Anderson, *Trapped by Success*, xiii–xiv.

In 1961, John F. Kennedy assumed the office of the president and with it, the residual obligations of his predecessor. The fear of communist aggression coming from Moscow and Beijing was still prevalent in main stream America, and yet there was substantial apprehension regarding the potential measures required to deter it. President Kennedy held similar personal concerns about communist expansion, so his desire to remain faithful to a containment policy seems reasonable.

Remaining relatively loyal to a predecessor's policies has been a historically safe course of action. The abandonment of established norms and policies has seldom been seen as a way to preserve political office—unless these policies clearly demanded immediate change. So from a sheer professional point of view, it stands to reason that with regard to Vietnam, Kennedy would continue along a decisional path similar to Eisenhower's. Accordingly, Kennedy was reluctant to make any decisively aggressive moves in the region, but yet he understood the consequences of inaction.

At the time of Kennedy's inauguration, Viet Cong attacks in South Vietnam had become more frequent and of greater intensity. Compounding this threat was the almost immediate recognition that the southern forces were not adequately trained to repel (much less defeat) such aggression.[48] President Kennedy supposedly understood the insurgency threat better than Eisenhower and realized that a true defeat of communist aggression in the area would require not only "a military victory, but socioeconomic, political, and psychological victories as well."[49] Kennedy's response to the growing instability began to take a more robust military shape, but, still his approach was not that far removed from Eisenhower's. By maintaining a posture of containment, Kennedy remained committed to the policy of the previous administration. His methods however, would be more direct.

Kennedy saw special operations forces (SOF) as an essential tool in achieving success in the area. Although not requiring as large a logistical support network as conventional forces, SOF still needed unique reach-back capabilities best supported by PCMFs. This course of action facilitated force projection while the utilization of PCMFs

---

[48] "Vietnam and Its Wars: A Historical Overview of U.S. Involvement," *Looking Back on the Vietnam War,* ed. William Head and Lawrence Grinter (London: Greenwood Press, 1993), 25.

[49] Ibid.

in support provided discretion. By 1963, this vision would become strategy and perhaps more importantly, would frame many significant options and precedents for his successors. Kennedy was now committed to Vietnam, inextricably tied to its outcome through moral obligations and professional courtesy. By 1963, he had seen the turmoil in the area increase with violence and unpredictability. Coup attempts and civil discord were confronting U.S. forces there, and the expected responses required to mitigate further escalation were increasingly becoming less and less desirable. It is unknown, however, how Kennedy would have ultimately responded to the changing dynamics had his presidency not been cut short by an assassin's bullet.[50]

The assassination of President Kennedy did not change the fact that Vietnam remained an unanswered dilemma for the United States and that the instability in the South remained a strategic concern. Kennedy had reluctantly continued the policy of containment but had chosen rather unique methods—mainly the application of special operations forces. Lyndon Johnson also remained consistent with the previous administration's commitment to Vietnam, but he had bolder plans for a solution. His decisions, unlike his predecessors, seemed driven by events beyond strategic assessments. Johnson's sense of urgency leads to a second causal factor, and perhaps the strongest one, in explaining why PCMFs emerged in earnest in Vietnam—that personalities, political favors, and informal business relationships strongly influenced presidential decisions.

2. Unethical, Professional Relationships

If the consistency theory explains the continuum of policies through informal and formal measures of influence, then personalities and informal business practices could best explain presidential decisions made often in direct opposition to previously accepted methods. This factor most strongly represents the presidency of Lyndon B. Johnson.

When Johnson became President, Robert Caro notes, "the number of American troops—advisors, not combatants—in Vietnam was 16,000," and public interest was still

---

[50] Hess, *South Vietnam*, 150–53.

relatively small.[51] Johnson, like Kennedy, seemed poised to continue with the consistency theory when he pledged no wider war. But Johnson's actions were in direct opposition to his words, and by 1966—only a little over two years after his inauguration—there were 385,000 U.S. troops involved in the conflict. In fact, in perhaps the most telling statistic, Caro points out that "by the end of 1966, more Americans had died *in* Vietnam than had been in Vietnam when Johnson became President."[52] Such a tremendous separation between deeds and words framed Johnson's presidency and brought to light the lengths that he would take to preserve (or more accurately, improve) his political position.

Caro describes Johnson as a "genius in the art of politics,"[53] and his *Means of Ascent* offers a detailed critique into Johnson's deft political maneuverings and back-road Texas business deals. Johnson used whatever means necessary to gain advantages, to defeat political rivals, and to return financial favors. Often times these dealings stirred significant questions from the media about Johnson's ethical decision making and business practices. Seemingly, however, Johnson was always able to quell these doubts through various means of influence. Perhaps no source of influence in the Johnson camp was greater than that wielded by Brown & Root, a giant in the Texas construction business. Caro's work provides a substantial account of this influence and of Johnson's personal relationship with the Brown Brothers—Herman and George—owners and operators of Brown & Root.

Caro reports that Brown & Root "had lavishly poured money into his [Johnson's] campaigns" and had become the single largest financial contributor throughout LBJ's political career.[54] The Brown brothers donated "hundreds of thousands of dollars" to Johnson's campaigns, beginning with his aspirations to become a member of the House

---

[51] Robert Caro, *Means of Ascent, The Years of Lyndon Johnson* (New York: Random House, 1990), xxiii.

[52] Ibid., xxiv

[53] Ibid., xxxi.

[54] Ibid., 13. *Also*, interestingly, in 1966, Donald Rumsfeld, then congressman of Illinois, condemned contracts between KBR and the government during the Vietnam War, stating, "Why this huge contract has not been and is not now being adequately audited is beyond me. The potential for waste and profiteering under such a contract is substantial." Pratap Chatterjee, Halliburton's Army: The Way America Makes War, Speech at Powell's City of Books (Feb. 18, 2009). *See, also,* Yasin, *Playing Catch–Up*, 460.

of Representatives and culminating with his rise to the presidency. In return, Johnson made Brown & Root wealthy. This *quid pro quo* relationship was undoubtedly critical to Johnson's political campaign successes and gave a private company unlimited access to, and unprecedented influence over, the President of the United States. Caro sums this up best in the following:

> Through federal contracts, Johnson had made (Herman) Brown rich, and given him the chance to build the huge projects of which he had long dreamed, and Brown had ordered up contributions from dozens of subcontractors on Brown & Root dams and highways and had, in giving from his own firm's coffers, gone to the edge of the law, and some Internal Revenue Service agents were later to contend, over that edge into the realm of fraud in order to finance Lyndon Johnson's ambition.[55]

The two Texas entities—Brown & Root and Lyndon Johnson—were inextricably linked, each one recognizing the value of the other. An example of this recognition can be seen from Johnson's decision on whether or not to run for the Senate in 1942. "Herman's younger brother George delivered to Johnson his brother's pledge: if Lyndon wanted to run in 1942, the money would be available again—all that was needed."[56] The influence of Brown & Root upon Johnson's early political career was indisputable and its influence continued throughout his presidency despite Johnson's claims to the contrary.[57] George Brown became a trusted confidante of LBJ, and "whenever Brown visited Washington, Johnson made the suave contractor part of the inner circle."[58]

Brown & Root, having financed Johnson from the 1940s and into his election as Vice President, was rewarded after Kennedy's assassination with lucrative contracts in the escalating Vietnam War. Business journalist Dan Briody has written: "Johnson, who became president in 1963 after Kennedy's assassination and who was elected with broad support in 1964, used the Gulf of Tonkin incident, in order to justify the sending of

---

[55] Caro, *Means of Ascent*, 16.

[56] Ibid.

[57] Although Caro's book does not address LBJ's presidency specifically, there are implicit conclusions drawn that Johnson knew he would, at least publicly, need to distance himself from Brown & Root

[58] Caro, *Means of Ascent*, 15. Additionally, Edward A. Clark, a powerful lawyer and former Texas Secretary of State, and who – in 1982, was still identified as "one of the twenty most powerful Texans" – served for over twenty years as Lyndon Johnson and Brown & Root's lawyer. Ibid., 56.

ground troops into Vietnam. The result of that move was the need for billions of dollars' worth of bases, airstrips, ports, and bridges. Enter Brown & Root."[59]

In 1965, a year after Johnson stepped up America's participation in Vietnam, Brown & Root joined three other construction and project management behemoths, Raymond International, Morris-Knudsen, and J.A. Jones to form one of the largest civilian-based military construction conglomerates in history. That team of corporations "literally changed the face of Vietnam, clearing out wide swaths of jungle for airplane landing strips, dredging channels for ships, and building American bases from Da Nang to Saigon."[60]

The nature of LBJ's relationship to Brown & Root can best be described in one word: corrupt. Magnifying this corruption were LBJ's deceptive intentions and his dominating personality. Johnson was a man who believed that he had to deter communism in Southeast Asia while advancing his ultimate goal of a Great Society. To do this he needed to convince the American public of one thing while doing something altogether different. This sleight of hand would come to be known as Johnson's "credibility gap"—a politically correct term for Johnson's deceitfulness. The credibility gap underlines an even larger deceit, which was Johnson's personal relationship with Brown & Root and the financial favors he owed them. As Jeffrey Helsing points out: "Just as the American public and Congress were deceived, so too, were the domestic and economic planners in Johnson's administration kept in the dark about … Vietnam."[61] This pattern of deceit contributed to the third causal argument—that Congress seemed unprepared to effectively question, much less counter, Johnson's actions, perhaps, because, arguably, Congress had little proficiency in understanding, much less supervising, hastily contracted PCMFs within a theater of war on such a large scale.

---

[59] Dan Briody, *The Halliburton Agenda, The Politics of Oil and Money* (New Jersey: John Wiley and Sons, 2004), 163–4.

[60] Ibid., 164.

[61] Jeffrey W. Helsing, *Johnson's War/Johnson's Great Society, The Guns and Butter Trap* (Westport, CT: Praeger Publishers, 2000), x.

3.   An Unprepared Congress

Confident politician that he was, Johnson knew that to succeed both abroad and domestically, he would need to wage war with unprecedented tools. Meanwhile, Brown & Root, always eager to earn a profit, was more than willing to offer up its services in support of the war. Brown & Root had capabilities beyond that of the current military and more importantly, by employing them in theater, Johnson would free up critical military manpower necessary for the task of war fighting. By steering lucrative construction contracts towards George Brown, Johnson was able to swiftly and decisively establish the necessary logistical requirements of a long-term military engagement while being able to publicly profess support for the American servicemen in Vietnam—a method that put unavoidable pressure on Congress (at least initially) to allocate and apportion funds.

Congress was ill-prepared to oversee Johnson's ability to mobilize swiftly the support of Brown & Root, largely due to the close personal nature Johnson held with the company. Although there is historical evidence of war profiteering by only a select few companies, it is hard to determine whether this occurred through the same personal interactions as exhibited by Johnson and Brown & Root.[62]

Additionally, the impacts that emerged PCMFs (like Brown & Root) had on the budget were significant as increases in military spending were much higher than expected.[63] As economist Murray Weidenbaum noted, "The Government would increase its orders in September, October, November of 1965, no reflection whatsoever in any current budget, but those orders were obviously immediately escalating the economy."[64]

---

[62] Several works exist that discuss companies gaining substantial profit from war-time contracts. For example David Kennedy in *Freedom from Fear*, states: "in WWII, General Motors had one-tenth of all war production, two-thirds of all prime contracts went to only one hundred companies, and thirty three of the largest corporations had one-half of all contracts." David Kennedy, *Freedom from Fear: The American People in Depression and War, 1929-1945* (New York: Oxford University Press, 1999), 621-22. This implies that the big corporations were able to position themselves to reap the biggest benefits. The "rich get richer" sentiment is echoed by R. Elberton Smith in *The Army and Economic Mobilization* (Washington D.C.: Office of the Chief of Military History, Department of the Army, 1959), passim. This thesis contends that although a select percentage of large companies have certainly benefited from war none seem to have done so from the almost untraceable, direct personal arrangements established by Johnson.

[63] Helsing, *Johnson's War*, 193.

[64] Murray Weidenbaum, testimony during Joint Economic Committee Hearings on *The Economic Effect of Vietnam Spending*, April 27, 1967, 184, quoted in Helsing, *Johnson's War*, 193.

Weidenbaum noted, "that a key factor to watch was new obligations, which includes both government payrolls and contracts with private firms;"[65] "The actual amount of new obligations incurred during fiscal year 1966 was somewhat in excess of $67 billion or almost one-fourth greater than in 1965. Actual expenditures increased at a much slower rate during the same period—17 percent. In other words, obligations are the more sensitive lead indicator."[66]

The fact that Congress seemed to be unaware and, more specifically, unwilling to confront Johnson's political intentions created an environment conducive to the personal whims of the president and the financial aspirations of Brown & Root and other private military companies it helped to bring along. To make matters worse, public sentiment was becoming increasingly hostile towards U.S. involvement in Vietnam. Protests began to surface with increasing regularity questioning why American forces were there. Congress was becoming entangled with moral sentiments, constitutional entitlements, and its legislative authorities.[67] Consequently, the fourth and final causal variable—that often damning public opinion caused U.S. leaders to operate with political recklessness.

4.   Public Opinion

Public opinion, seemingly inconsequential to Johnson's motives during the initial phase of his presidency, had taken a heavy toll. And as Johnson's presidency limped towards its inglorious end, what to do with Vietnam became the primary campaign topic in 1968. Republican candidate Richard Nixon pledged to withdraw American forces from Vietnam through a policy he eventually called "Vietnamization"—a process that would put Vietnamese officials in the lead in developing and maintaining their own government infrastructure and means of security. But Nixon, much like his predecessor, was very adept in deception and knew that the policy of Vietnamization was intended to sway public opinion in support of his administration. Nixon knew that, in reality, to succeed where others had failed he would have to drastically (recklessly, in some

---

[65] Helsing, *Johnson's War*, 193.

[66] Center for Strategic Studies, *Economic Impact of the Vietnam War*, 34, quoted in Helsing, *Johnson's War*, 193.

[67] Komer, *Bureaucracy at War*, 81–88.

regards) increase the aggressive perception and resolve of the United States. Nixon professed a "madman theory" in the hopes that he would convince the Northern communist leaders that he was wholly unpredictable and that he considered the utilization of nuclear weapons as a viable option.[68]

Ironically, the public decree of seeking Vietnamization while privately conveying a madman persona to communist leaders set the conditions for a continuance of profiteering by the private military companies. George Brown no longer had a well-compensated ally in the Oval Office, but his company had grown immensely, and its contributions to the Vietnam War—at least logistically—were intrinsically tied to the force projection capabilities of all manner of combat forces. Air strips, bases, roads, supply points, etc., were all critical nodes in military missions that would facilitate Nixon's madman approach. Additionally, the technical expertise required to operate efficiently could not be guaranteed without the likes of General Dynamics and other large companies. Hostile public (and, now, congressional) opinion encouraged Nixon to rely privately on the assets and capabilities of the private military companies in theater.[69]

Nixon's public deceit declaring that the Vietnamese will determine their own future—but privately waging aggressive military operations may have in actuality prolonged the war.[70] Ironically, by prolonging U.S. involvement—and in some regards altogether increasing it—Nixon may have inadvertently made the rise and subsequent role of the PCMF much more lucrative than it had been. Further, the precedents set by Johnson and Nixon during the Vietnam War potentially revealed how much influence PCMFs can have on presidential decisions.

The previous section presented evidence that the issues, conditions, and decisions made during the Vietnam era may have set significant precedents regarding PCMF utilization. Although Vietnam was indeed an atypical conflict, this section argues that

---

[68] Jeffrey Kimball, *Nixon's Vietnam War* (Lawrence, KS: University Press, 1998), 23. Nixon's madman theory was predicated on his desire to project an image of an unconventional and unpredictable leader with a nuclear arsenal to the North Vietnamese. He, essentially, was gambling with the North, hoping that they would meet his demands (or at least compromise extensively) in order to protect their society from a nuclear attack.

[69] Kimball, *Nixon's Vietnam War*, 213–36.

[70] Ibid., 371.

that was only in the historical sense. Vietnam ushered in the asymmetrical threat and all the ambiguity that comes with it. Fighting no clearly defined belligerent with fluctuating objectives in the midst of opaque presidential motives would, in this author's opinion, set the conditions for PCMF exploitation some forty years later.

C.   EXPANDING THE "CREDIBILITY GAP": FROM LBJ TO TODAY

The credibility gap mentioned earlier in this chapter was indicative of President Johnson's powerful public persona mixed with his personal belief in his own infallibility. But the credibility gap did not end with Johnson's administration. Over the last ten years, the demands of OIF and OEF have certainly generated their own credibility concerns, e.g., accusations of favoritism and profiteering certainly surrounded Vice President Cheney and his ties to Halliburton. The military has not been immune either, as its lucrative contracts to all manner of PCMFs seemed to reveal a system in which the military was far too closely connected to forces many considered nothing more than mercenaries. The former accusation was (and still is) never far removed from discussion about the Bush Administration, while the latter was and is still hotly debated. This section will focus on the latter contention and will provide reasons why the manner in which the U.S. has chosen to fight, i.e., COIN, has produced an inescapable environment conducive to privatized exploitation.

1.   The Unfortunate "Truisms"[71] of COIN

America did not win in Vietnam because the U.S. faced an opponent who fought an asymmetrical war—combining conventional methods with unconventional ones. The Vietnamese RVN and the VC frustrated the endeavors of American combat forces. Now, similar methods are being employed in Afghanistan and were, just recently, used successfully by insurgents in Iraq. The difficulty in fighting an asymmetrical war comes in not just understanding who your enemy is but why he has chosen to engage you.

---

[71] I am referring here to the works of Army Colonel, Paul Yingling, who published the article *A Failure of Generalship* in a 2007 issue of the Armed Forces Journal. Col Yingling has said on more than one occasion that senior military leaders speaking in "truisms" rather than the truth is a disservice to civilian leadership. See, http://www.csmonitor.com/USA/Military/2012/0206/Reports-on-Afghanistan-war-too-rosy-Army-officer-others-say-yes/(page)/2.

Without fully grasping the operational environment, the former becomes difficult, the latter, impossible. For this reason, Counterinsurgency, or COIN, became the method of choice for U.S. ground forces during Vietnam and later, OIF and OEF. COIN implies that understanding the enemy is key, but leveraging support of his surrounding population, essential. By winning the population—commonly referred to as "winning the hearts and minds," the enemy is denied safe-haven and thus, rendered combat ineffective. Winning hearts and minds is accomplished through various civil affairs initiatives aimed at establishing or, where applicable, improving basic humanitarian needs. As these needs are met, the initiatives follow along a progressive evolution, becoming more complex until all basic requirements of a functioning community can be met[72]—at least with enough integrity to operate their basic functions. These seem reasonable to accomplish, in theory, but in practice have become so misunderstood and misallocated that seldom is a sequential path established. Far too often, an immediate jump from basic needs to building a complex, networked infrastructure has occurred. Tactically, this is a tragedy, as the complex initiatives will seldom see completion while more pressing needs are ignored. This is especially true in austere regions of Afghanistan and Iraq, where local, tribally–based communities simply need basic necessities like food and water but instead are far too often promised loftier initiatives. Power grids and school systems are important, yes. But their completion runs secondary to basic humanitarian supplies. To make matters worse, if these lofty objectives are not completed, or are done so in shoddy fashion, it can actually damage any fledgling relationship and turn the local population against the Americans; fostering a belief that the Westerners cannot meet their own promises, or worse, that they refuse to see the populations' plight.

This section does not mean to imply that COIN is a useless approach, but it does suggest that it is a fallible one. In the U.S. military's rush to push the benefits of a COIN campaign, they have created a system that rewards a high operational tempo with swift results, but unfortunately, implies unrealistic expectations. The machination of this behavior is easy to identify in U.S. forces that are operating (deployed) on a finite timeline, as tangible results equal operational relevance.

---

[72] *See*, Maslow's Hierarchy of Needs.

COIN is not social-engineering, but it can be mistaken for such when misapplied. It is an applicable tool, but like all tools it has its place. Utilizing COIN tactics in areas that are not fully understood can have unintended consequences. It is imperative that all leaders understand that COIN is not a universal method and should not be considered as the default alternative when entering into a new environment. Across the board, military leaders should not be entering into discussions with an open wallet. This erodes respect, fosters corruption, and may, in the long run, create dependencies where none existed. This complete inability (or refusal) to grasp the concept that infusing an operational environment with U.S. money and energy before fully understanding it may be doing more harm than good. But this lack of judgment is not wholly the fault of the military. Agencies such as the DoS, USAID, Provincial Reconstruction Teams (PRTs), and various types of NGOs, often fail to assist in synchronizing their efforts. Worse still, some or all of these entities have proven guilty of funding projects that do not seem in accordance with a population's needs. Thankfully, these are exceptions and not the rule, but the truth is, it does not take a lot of exceptions for a local population to feel that the U.S. is operating in its own best interests. This, ultimately, helps an enemy continuously recruit from a population that sees American initiatives sorely out of touch with Arab culture.

Furthermore, the "truisms" of COIN are just as overly abused by today's politicians as they were during the Vietnam era. For example, often quoted phrases like "the situation is delicate, but improving," or, the fate of the [Vietnamese/Iraqis/Afghanis] will be decided by them not us," to "we are turning the corner, but there is more work to be done," all say something without saying anything—speaking in "truisms" rather than the truth. COIN by its very nature, provides politicians with ample wiggle room since, unlike the stark contrast of battling belligerents, it focuses on the entirely gray area of civic improvements and strategic partnerships. The latitude that COIN provides politicians and senior military commanders alike is unfortunate because it does not effectively hold them to task, since the task is never clearly understood.

The fallacy of COIN is that it is purposefully ambiguous in both direction and intent. Such an opaque operational environment, with agencies across the board operating disjointedly and with no definitive objective, is ripe for exploitation by the PMI. PCMFs will naturally want to capitalize on the legal ambiguity and operational confusion, providing profitable services either wholly outside military expertise, i.e., civil-construction efforts, or as an augmenting entity during political discourse. Either way, ironically, the U.S.'s insistence on following a controversial method of "fighting" seems destined to continue a course of lucrative contracts and skeptical motives. Vietnamization was the beginning of COIN. OIF and OEF have seen it mature.

Conclusion

Vietnam was certainly an atypical conflict, and it presented several prominent world leaders with an interesting array of political, military, religious, and socio-economic quandaries that have been thoroughly dissected by scholars in the field. This chapter has advanced a relatively new topic, on which there is still scant literature, and concludes that the rise of privately contracted military firms—at least as we know them today—began in earnest in Vietnam. Two separate sections were devoted to this cause. In the first section, four causal variables were presented for why the Vietnam War was the catalyst for PCMF influence and integration. First, the consistency theory presented the conditions for Kennedy and Johnson to continue the containment policy credited to President Eisenhower, and thus began perhaps an unavoidable course of escalation. Second, the unethical professional relationships of President Johnson spawned the tremendous influence of Brown & Root and made privatizing elements of war fighting extremely lucrative for logistically and technically specialized companies (as well as for politically savvy businessmen). Third, an unprepared Congress encouraged a vicious cycle of funding, distributing lucrative contracts to elements that the legislative branch did not have the proficiency to oversee. And fourth, a growingly hostile U.S. public opinion regarding Vietnam encouraged the administrations of the era to continue force projection, distribution of aid, and civic-support initiatives outside the public view. Any one of these four factors could feasibly justify the emergence of PCMFs, but when viewed together, these four causal variables produce an environment that is ripe for exploitation.

In the second section, this chapter proposes that the same "credibility gap" that plagued Johnson's legacy resurfaced during the Bush Administration since scrutiny and skepticism still surround VP Cheney and Halliburton as well as the massive amount of contracts awarded to controversial PCMFs, e.g., Blackwater. The chapter concludes with a theoretical discussion of COIN, tying the origin of modern-day COIN to "Vietnamization" and highlighting the fact that the U.S.'s reliance on COIN may be fostering a reliance on PCMFs. This sets the conditions for Chapter III—the case study of Operation Iraqi Freedom.

IV.   THE UNITED STATES AND PCMFS IN MODERN WARFARE—CASE STUDY: OPERATION IRAQI FREEDOM

Iraq presents an opportunity of a lifetime.[73]

Privatized services have always been vital to the U.S. military's ability to project farther, faster, and for sustained durations, to a greater extent than that of their enemies. This is perhaps to be expected from an industrialized nation with a capitalist economy. But, as we saw in the preceding chapter, Vietnam pushed the civilian sector's relationship with the military into one of intrinsic commitment. The profits obtained by both communities (military and privatized) were simply too lucrative to abandon. For the next several decades, PCMFs would continue to emerge, finding their own niche in the contracting network. This network had substantial influence domestically but its global reach was still maturing. It would take an expansive, international event to really get the ball rolling. Enter the end of the Cold War. When the Soviet Union collapsed, the contracting network expanded exponentially as satellite countries of the former Soviet Regime instantly needed almost all conceivable forms of customizable, tactical and operational, civil-military support. PCMFs were able to meet these needs, and thus continued to grow, both in number and capabilities, and to establish firm footholds in the international market.

Between the 1990s and the early 2000s PCMFs, although distinguishable by services provided, had, collectively, grown into a formidable force. By 2001, PCMFs numbered in the hundreds[74] and their growth showed no signs of slowing down. It is difficult to ascertain any singular reason for PCMF growth during this period. Although, certainly, Post-Cold War opportunities played a role, so too did domestic, federal job

---

[73] Rahman Saifur, "Call to Take Advantage of Opportunities in Iraq," *Gulf News* (Dubai, United Arab Emirates), April 21, 2004. Quoted in Jeremy Scahill, *Blackwater*, 219.

[74] This is subjective, at best, as there is no agency or organization responsible for keeping track of the numbers of PCMFs.

reductions, as well as a drawdown in U.S. armed forces.[75] If, like most scholarly work, we recognize that a confluence of conditions drove PCMF growth,[76] then a second expansive event would place it into overdrive. Enter, September 11, 2001.

Nine-eleven (9/11) was (and still is) a polarizing event. Although occurring on U.S. soil, the event would have global impact. The U.S. declared a named enemy—Al Qaeda, and a named threat—terrorism. The new "war on terror" would be fought with every measure at U.S. disposal. PCMFs would not only be necessary in this war, but essential, as America's projection into Afghanistan, followed by Iraq, would need to be swift and decisive with the ability to sustain U.S. endeavors indefinitely.

This chapter will focus on the latter of these two wars—Iraq, up to and including 2011—and will offer evidence as to the applicability and necessity of the PCMFs operating there. The chapter is divided into two parts. Part one will present statistical data on the makeup and dispersion of PCMFs in theater, focusing on a macro view of civilian-military operations and tactical compatibility. Presenting evidence that fighting a war without PCMF assistance is now inconceivable. Part two will note the necessities of PCMFs but demonstrate that contractors in Iraq became a polarizing issue, testing the boundaries of civil-military relations. This will be supported through the dissection of particular type of PCMF, and the one which seems the most controversial, i.e., the MSDF—commonly referred to as the Private Security Company, or PSC.

A.   USE OF PCMFS IN THEATER

It had started small, a byproduct of all the mistakes at the beginning: not enough troops, ignoring the insurgency, starting reconstruction prematurely. Soon they were everywhere: guarding the diplomats, the generals, military bases the size of small cities, and thousands of supply convoys filled with guns and ammunition and food. Suddenly no one and no thing could move around Iraq without them. Some human rights groups had mercs [mercenaries]. The media had mercs. The International

---

[75] From 1990-1997 the U.S. military reduced its total manpower from 2,043,705 to 1,438,562, "Selected Manpower Statistics Fiscal Year 1990," AD-A235 849, Washington Headquarters Services, Directorate for Information Operations and Reports, Department of Defense. Data for 1997 is available at http://siadapp.dmdc.osd mil/personnel/MILITARY/history/tab9.

[76] I am thinking here of Dr. Thomas C. Bruneau's description of "a diverse set of drivers," "Contracting Out Security," Paper written for Department of National Security Affairs, Naval Postgraduate School, Monterey, CA. (2011), 8.

Republican Institute, chaired by John McCain, and the National Democratic Institute, chaired by Madeleine Albright, used mercs to spread democracy. The Iraqi politicians had them full time and the American politicians had them whenever came through to find out how the war was going. The market was so hot it became known as the "Iraq Bubble." The demand to be safe never stopped, so neither did the supply. The mercs came from the Army, Navy, Air Force, Marines, from small-town police departments and the LAPD. And form other nations' armies: the British SAS, the Australian Defence Forces, the Nepalese Gurkhas. One Peruvian I met swore that there were ex-members of the Shining Path in Iraq, the terrorists who massacred thusands of peasants during the eighties and nineties. Terrorists fighting terrorists.[77]

PCMFs would flourish in Iraq for a number of reasons but the foundation for their expansion there would be based on the initial lack U.S. troops. With troops already committed to Afghanistan, the Army was stretched thin. DoD was forced to look for ways to increase combat related specialties without reinstituting the draft. PCMFs not only filled the gaps, they also came at significantly lower political costs, as the Administration could utilize them without affecting public opinion—at least not to the same degree as calling for more soldiers. PCMFs were expected to provide substantial enhancement while mitigating public perception. What was unexpected however, was the absolute reliance that the U.S. government would come to have on PCMF provisions.

The United States has used contractors quite extensively during previous military operations, as already evidenced in the two previous chapters, but the ratio between contractors and members of the armed services in Iraq is roughly 2.5 times higher than any other major conflict.[78] This disparity in ratio remained relatively constant throughout the Iraq War, even during the troop surge of 2007, to the drawdown of troops beginning in 2009 (see Figure 1).[79] Interestingly, "according to DOD, as of March 2011, there were

---

[77] Steve Fainaru, *Big Boy Rules: America's Mercenaries Fighting in Iraq* (Philiadelphia, PA: De Capo Press, 2008), 22-23.

[78] Congressional Budget Office (CBO), Contractors' Support of U.S. Operations in Iraq, August 2008, 1.

[79] Department of Defense Contractors in Iraq and Afghanistan: 2011 Background and Analysis, accessed through http://www.fas.org/sgp/crs/natsec/R40764.pdf.

approximately 64,000 DOD contractor personnel in Iraq compared to 46,000 uniformed personnel in-country. Contractors made up approximately 58% of DOD's workforce in Iraq."[80]

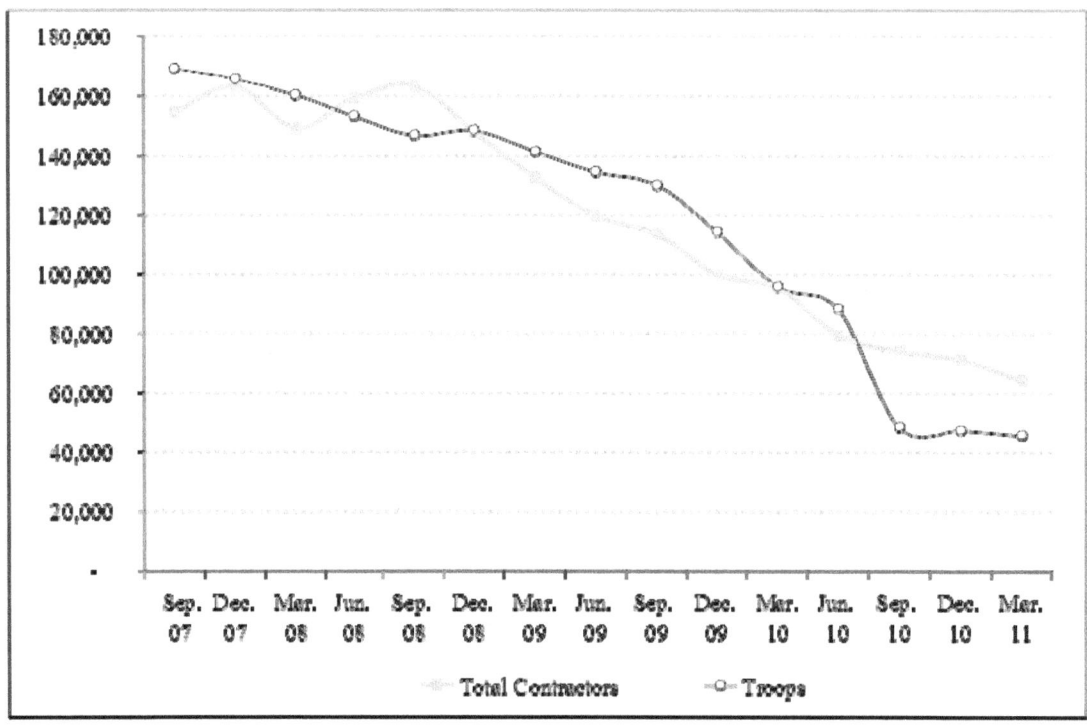

Source: CENTCOM Quarterly Census Reports; Joint Staff, Joint Chiefs of Staff, "Boots on the Ground" monthly reports to Congress.

Notes: The y-intercept for the level of troops and contractor personnel is similar. The R^2 value for the linear trend line for contractor personnel is 0.93 and for uniformed personnel is .91. R^2 is a statistical term used to describe the goodness of the fit between the trend line and the data points. R^2 is a descriptive measure between 0 and 1. The closer the R^2 value is to one, the better the fit of the trend line to the data.

Figure 1. Number of Contractor Personnel in Iraq vs. Troop Levels (From Department of Defense Contractors in Afghanistan and Iraq: Background and Analysis, 2011).

Contracted security often gets the lion's share of attention—mainly due to the mercenary stigma—but, in reality, the MLFs and MSFs (identified in Chapter I) are, in number, the predominate source of contractors in Iraq, require the largest portion of the budget, and perform a range of services so diverse and so specialized that the military quite frankly cannot operate without them. "As of March 2011, approximately 39,000

---

[80] Department of Defense Contractors in Iraq and Afghanistan: 2011 Background and Analysis, accessed through http://www.fas.org/sgp/crs/natsec/R40764.pdf.

personnel (61% of contractors) performed base support functions such as maintaining the grounds, running dining facilities, and performing laundry services (see Figure 8). Security was the second most common service provided, with approximately 10,500 personnel (16% of contractors). Combined, these two categories accounted for almost 80% of DOD contractors in Iraq"[81] (see Figure 2).[82]

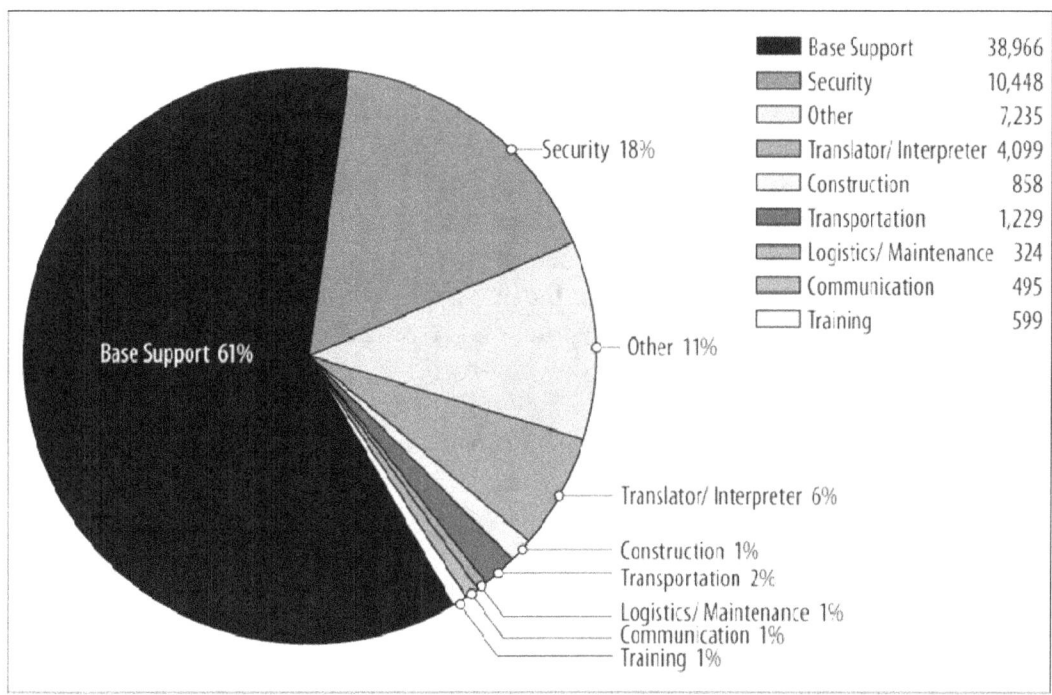

Source: DOD US CENTCOM 2ⁿᵈ Quarter FY2011 Contractor Census Report.

Notes: Numbers may vary slightly from data in other sections of the report due to differences in the points in time when data was gathered. The Department of Defense did not separately track Logistics/Maintenance or Training until the first quarter of 2010.

Figure 2.   Contractor Personnel in Iraq by Type of Service Provided
            (As of March, 2011), (From Department of Defense Contractors in
            Afghanistan and Iraq: Background and Analysis, 2011).

[81] DoD, Contractors, http://www.fas.org/sgp/crs/natsec/R40764.pdf.

[82] Ibid.

The relationship between PCMFs and the DoD has become so intertwined that ratio of PCMFs to troops on the ground is directly related to the current mission of the armed services. For example, in a 2009 report on contractors in Iraq, The Department of Defense stated that:

> As the overall number of troops in Iraq has decreased, so too has the overall number of contractors. For example, since June 2008, as troop levels dropped by approximately 108,000 (70%), total contractors fell by approximately 95,000 (60%). However, the number of contractors did not decrease uniformly across the contractor workforce. For example, during the same period, contractors providing base support and construction declined by 57% (51,000 personnel) and 98% (35,000 personnel) respectively, whereas the number of contractors providing security actually increased by 14% (1,000 personnel). This data indicates that as the services required by DOD change during the course of operations, the percentages and numbers of contractors providing different types of services also change. The drop in the number of contractor personnel performing base support and construction is a reflection of DOD's shrinking footprint and winding down of reconstruction activities. The percentage of contractors performing base support has remained relatively constant, the percentage working in construction has decreased, and the percentage performing security has increased.[83]

A separate but interesting point of observation is the low numbers of local nationals hired as contractors in Iraq, despite the emphasis by senior leaders to do otherwise.[84] This seems counterintuitive to the prospects of COIN, in that the local population seems separated from the prospects of being rewarded contracts that would ease economic hardship—at least in isolated fashion. The evidence presented in Table 2 runs corollary to the author's theory presented in Chapter II, i.e., without a full understanding of how to employ COIN tactics, the wrong target population may benefit, making the operational (and political) environment harder to leverage.

---

[83] DoD, Contractors in Iraq, http://www.fas.org/sgp/crs/natsec/R40764.pdf

[84] General Raymond T. Odierno, Memorandum, Increased Employment of Iraq Citizens Through Command Contracts, Multi-National Force-Iraq, January 31, 2009.

Table 2.   Contractor Personnel in Iraq (as of March, 2011) (From Department of
Defense Contractors in Afghanistan and Iraq: Background and Analysis,
2011).

	Total Contractors	U.S. Citizens	Third-Country Nationals	Local Nationals
Number	64,253	18,595	36,423	9,337
Percent of Total	100%	29%	57%	14%

Source: CENTCOM 2nd Quarter FY2011 Contractor Census Report. Percentages do not equal 100% due to rounding.

Wars are never cheap—whether in lives, resources, or capital, and OIF was no exception. The numbers of personnel listed throughout the preceding figures and tables are indicative of an unprecedented amount of financial capital, especially considering that contracting out through privatized companies cost an exceptional percentage of the overall budget. DOD obligated approximately $15.4 billion on contracts in the Iraq Theater of operations in FY2010, representing 20% of total spending in those regions.[85] From FY2005 to FY2010, DOD obligated approximately $112.8 billion on contracts primarily in the Iraq Theater of operations, representing 19% of total obligations for operations in Iraq.[86]

1.   Supporting or Eroding U.S. Forces?

The Military Industrial Complex that Eisenhower warned about is now in full effect. Privatization of military-centric provisions is such an integral part of how the U.S. goes to war today that outsourcing services goes largely unnoticed. Through conditions, precedents, and opportunities, PCMFs have established a niche for themselves as an unavoidable necessity and there seems to be no end in sight. To make matter worse—or better, depending on your point of view—PCMFs have the luxury of recruiting from a virtually limitless pool. The symbiotic relationship between PCMFs and the military

---

[85] Based on total obligations of $76.6 billion. Data includes total war-related obligations by year incurred (with classified request based on appropriations), based on data provided by the Defense Finance and Accounting Service. Classified appropriations allocated 60% to Iraq operations and 40% to Afghanistan operations. See CRS Report RL33110, *The Cost of Iraq, Afghanistan, and Other Global War on Terror Operations Since 9/11*, by Amy Belasco.

[86] Ibid. Based on total obligations of $588.6 billion. The percentage of contract expenditures for operations in Iraq from FY2005 through FY2010 were 24%, 23%, 15%,17%, 20%, and 20%, respectively.

means that military members are routinely exposed to the pay and benefits bestowed upon U.S. contractors. This is often an enticing incentive for those seeking post-military careers.[87]

In addition to highly competitive pay, contractors are not held to the same standards of the military. There are no set rules of behavior outside what may be stipulated in the contract, and punitive measures are rarely as severe as those enacted under the Uniform Code of Military Justice (UCMJ). [88] This can be another enticing factor and encourages a departure from the military ranks. Furthermore, contractors have, by design, an exceptional amount of latitude to carry out their mission. This means that they are not confined to operational boundaries and, therefore, can expand their mission based on real-world occurrences, not prescribed phase lines or templates which can severely hinder military operations.

There is no doubt that PCMFs play a tremendous part in supporting U.S. military operations, but they may also be causing a "brain-drain" on the military ranks. The PMI is a ready and willing recipient of those with valuable military skill sets and because former military members enter the private sector with extensive training, they are immediately mission capable. This means that PCMFs rarely have to develop training programs to get their new employees up to speed—creating a mutually beneficial and sustainable system.

In *The Market for Force*, Deborah Avant implies that all of the above assist the PCMF in growing more and more robust, but this growth (potentially) comes at a great cost to the military. Avant begins the discussion (to be advanced later in this chapter) that PCMFs may be testing the limits of civil-military relations from unprecedented angles. She summarizes this in the following:

> The blurring of lines between the military and [PCMFs] may also call into question the esteem with which Americans view the military, changing the value placed on military service, causing difficulties with military

---

[87] It would be interesting to compare PCMF proliferation with that of voluntary military separation. Although the author concedes this to be an extemporaneous study outside the intentions of this thesis, he nonetheless speculates that there is at least some corollary relationship.

[88] A contemporary theory exists that the UCMJ could serve as a control measure over private contractors. This is inappropriate however, and will be addressed in detail in Chapter VI.

recruitment and/or retention, and diminishing U.S. military effectiveness. Any of these could spur disruption and change that could feed into a disintegrative challenge to the control of force in the U.S.[89]

2. Operational Boundaries

OIF presented military commanders with unique challenges, none more important than the de-confliction of efforts between PCMFs and military ground forces. Although Afghanistan and, to some degree, other regional conflicts presented similar hurdles, Iraq was the first area to provided substantial exposure between PCMFs and the U.S. military in a highly complex, and often densely populated, urban environment. Further complicating the operational environment was, again, the insistence on COIN. COIN is hard enough to conduct in a U.S./host-nation environment, but when you add a third party to the mix, in this case PCMFs—who can simultaneously support DoS and DoD initiatives—you get a mixing bowl of directives and subsequent results. In order to mitigate this, both primary U.S. entities—contractors and the military—tried to separate themselves from one another, but this resulted in "stovepiped"[90] information and perhaps weakened operational efficiency. The mutually exclusive relationship between the two organizations made a theoretical boundary and often polarized opinions on both sides, sometimes going so far as to cause apprehension between the DoS and the DOD.

The lack of clearly defined operational boundaries only exacerbated the situation beyond the theoretical as both sides took separate viewpoints and measures of policing themselves.[91] Military commanders readily accept and expect operational boundaries in order to define their relative "battlespace"[92]—an area in which the ground commander

---

[89] Deborah D. Avant, *The Market for Force, The Consequences of Privatizing Security,*(New York: Cambridge University Press, 2007), 138.

[90] A common term in military lexicon that refers to an entity planning without external help or refusing—either knowingly or unknowingly—to share operationally advantageous information.

[91] Operational boundaries are agreed upon, graphical displays of an area of operation (AO). This area is usually depicted on a map and utilizes major terrain features, where available, as natural borders. This area is then "assigned" to a unit as their area of responsibility (AOR) and is an important step in establishing tactical and operational control.

[92] Among ground forces, it refers to the lowest level, tactical commander's immediate area. This usually denotes a battalion, commanded by a lieutenant colonel (LTC). Although it should be noted that there is an informal push to remove this term from discussions of COIN as it is not necessarily accurate in describing a commander's influence in an asymmetrical environment.

has ownership, i.e., responsibility for what happens. This ranges from the actions of his own unit, to those of host-nation forces, to even civilian incidents. Additionally, by having a defined battlespace, senior military leaders are much more readily able to identify what their subordinates are doing. Likewise, this instills in the subordinate a greater adherence to his mission and greater awareness of his actions and environment.

Military leaders readily accept geographical boundaries for other reasons as well. Since battlespace owners are clearly defined, each military commander can readily depict who is on his flank and easily de-conflict cross-boundary missions. At the highest levels, boundaries establish a common operating picture—an ability for the senior ranks to quickly grasp what is happening, why, and sometimes most importantly, to whom. This manner of battle tracking allows the commanders the ability to quickly re-allocate forces, shift operational focus, and/or dispatch immediate resources. Therefore, the establishment of operational boundaries is one of the very first measures taken upon receipt of deployment orders and is instrumental in establishing and maintaining command and control (C2) over any operational area—especially a combat zone, and perhaps even more so during contingency operations, where, without definitive control measures, the situation would be even more complex.

But PCMFs are not restrained by the operational control parameters of the military. Although PCMFs employ similar tactics in developing their projected areas of operations, they rarely share the information with military forces. This is especially true of MDSFs who operate security operations and protective services, often in a shroud of secrecy. As such, the battlespace can realistically contain U.S. armed forces with varying intentions and no cohesive methods of control.

OIF revealed the theoretical wall between PCMFs and military co-operability, coupled with the lack of any synchronized, tangible control measures. This meant that, in Iraq, highly trained U.S. armed forces with similar intent were acting mutually exclusively of one another. The fact that more incidents of fratricide or tactically damaging confrontations did not occur is testament to the tremendous leadership exercised by both parties. Control measures must be reformed so that, whether directly or indirectly, operational (and theoretical) boundaries can be clearly understood and synchronized. Sharing information and understanding one another's limitations go a long way towards maximizing efficiency. Failure to develop such reforms will continue to put U.S. personnel—and their mission—at odds with each other, unnecessarily.

3   Justifying Expenditures

There is substantial scholarly work and emerging analytical data surrounding the expenditures and funds spent in support of U.S. operations in Iraq.[93] Rather than simply re-present this data, this particular section will focus on the institutional arrangements which perhaps had greater impacts than previously suggested.

The need for greater fidelity in understanding operational boundaries was certainly a significant discovery during OIF, but so too was the amount of money spent there, and, perhaps more alarming, the lack of its supervision.[94] Three primary assumptions are made here. (1) That the U.S. lacked the expertise necessary to regulate its own contracts; (2) That PCMFs were able to exploit this inability; and, (3) that the lack of initial ground forces may have contributed to the DoD's ability to effectively utilize follow-on forces in a wider spectrum. Regardless, the U.S. was woefully unprepared for the amount of PCMF involvement in OIF—both in depth and scope.

The Commission on Wartime Contracting issued its final report in August, 2011 and declared that "at least $31 billion has been lost to contract waste and fraud"[95] but went on to speculate that this figure could be double. Although the report included both Iraq and Afghanistan, it points to a more serious concern—the lack of any substantial oversight.

---

[93] I am thinking here of the findings in the *2007 Commission on Army Acquisition and Program Management in Expeditionary Operations*, commonly referred to as *The Gansler Report*, as well as the Congressional Budget Office, and the Government Accounting Office, to name a few. All of these present ample evidence regarding specific financial expenditures, fraud, waste and abuse, and address current methodological inadequacies, but, in my opinion, fail to provide any substantial examination of the relationships between the civil-military institutions that may be contributing to extended contracts and a flawed way of doing business.

[94] Analysts have called the reliability of the DOD data into question. The Government Accountability Office revealed "that the DOD's quarterly contractor reports were not routinely checked for accuracy or completeness." Further, the DOD did not start collecting contractor data until the second half of 2007, despite employing contractors from the onset of operations. Additionally, keeping track of contractors is a tremendous challenge, as "contractors rotate in and out of theater more often than soldiers do." *See*, David Isenberg, *Shadow Force: Private Security Contractors in Iraq* (2009).

[95] CWC-NR-49, Wartime Contracting Commission final report to Congress, August, 2011, 1.

The use of PCMFs and contracting out services exploded in Iraq. But the comparative agencies/expertise designed to manage them did not. There was a tremendous amount of over reliance on contractors coupled with very little experienced supervision. The Commission found that the number of contract specialists, whose sole function was/is to oversee contingency contracting, rose by only three percent government-wide between 1992–2009, despite an enormous increase in contracting activity during that period.[96]

The justification for such an immense reliance on contracting out services falls somewhere between the government's needs (both the U.S. and Iraq) and the contractor's capabilities. In OIF, both the U.S. and Iraq needed multiple agencies to deal with security issues and civic concerns, simultaneously. This was largely outside the scope of influence of the force on the ground, especially considering the numbers of troops initially involved.[97] Although beyond the intent of this thesis, it is not unreasonable to hypothesize that the numbers of forces utilized during the invasion may have had indirect effects on the military's capabilities to exercise initiatives beyond their initial expectations. This becomes even more plausible considering that the DoD's obligations for contracts far outweighed those of other agencies.[98]

PCMFs were a quick solution to any operational gaps, as they offered customizable packages that could perform a wide variety of services. Perhaps even more important than their provisions, however, was what they meant to the numbers of uniformed personnel. PCMFs meant fewer troops were necessary—both during the invasion and later, during contingency operations. This is no small consideration and should be retained for further discussion, primarily because opponents of PCMFs believe their existence to be detrimental to good order and discipline but, I believe the opposite to be true. The military would need to produce and deploy well over one hundred thousand

---

[96] CWC-NR-49.

[97] Retired Army General Shinseki suggested in 2002, that he would like to have substantially more forces than the 150,000 desired by the former Secretary of Defense, Donald Rumsfeld. A source of contention between the two that resulted in Rumsfeld publicly announcing Shinseki's retirement eighteen months ahead of schedule.

[98] According to the CBO's report, from 2003-2007, DoD's $76 billion in contract obligations accounted for 90 percent of all dollars awarded. USAID and OSD were second and third, respectively.

additional troops to OIF alone if PCMFs were not part of the equation. That is a sobering statistic as it carries with it the very real problem of where these service members would come from. PCMFs are expensive to employ, certainly, but they are a much more politically palatable option than a request for an all-volunteer force to extend its deployment times in the face of two wars. Worse, the absence of PCMFs tables the discussion of reinstituting the draft. Barring a severe shift in current American ideology, this author believes the latter to be completely untenable.

While PCMFs potentially alleviate military personnel burdens they perhaps cause unnecessary financial obligations. This is primarily due to how PCMFs are contracted. While the primary methods of billing will be addressed in specifics later in this thesis, it should be noted here that the current arrangements seem conducive to the abuse mentioned in the The Gansler Report.[99]   KBR for example operates under a cost-plus contract which means the firm is paid for all of its allowed expenses to a set limit *plus* additional payment to allow for a profit.[100] If substantial consideration is not warranted to this type of arrangement, then mismanagement and corruption are strong possibilities.

B.   OPERATIONAL   CONFRONTATIONS   AND   STRATEGIC CONSEQUENCES

The concerns that were previously implied regarding boundaries, i.e., that there was little synchronization of effort and intent between PCMFs and the military in OIF, played themselves out on more than one occasion. Because boundaries were rarely de-

---

[99] *The Gansler Report* pointed the finger at the lack of quality trained personnel and methods, i.e., that there simply weren't enough contracting specialists and/or a system robust enough to oversee that appropriate methods of QA/QC were followed. The absence of either of these two produced an environment easily exploited. In order to address the discovered weaknesses, the report concluded with 4 recommendations:

    1. Increase the Stature, Quantity, and Career Development of the Army's Contracting Personnel, Military and Civilian (Especially for Expeditionary Operations), 47.

    2. Restructure Organization and Restore Responsibility to Facilitate Contracting and Contract Management in Expeditionary and CONUS Operations, 51.

    3. Provide Training and Tools for Overall Contracting Activities in Expeditionary Operations, 55.

    4. Obtain Legislative, Regulatory, and Policy Assistance to Enable Contracting Effectiveness in Expeditionary Operations, 56.

[100] Definition of cost-plus contracts accessed through Center for Strategic International Studies, http://csis.org/files/media/csis/pubs/081016_diig_cost_plus.pdf.

conflicted, if ever established, military forces and PCMFs often butted heads. Some of these encounters were rather mundane, nothing more than contractual disagreements or dissenting opinions regarding who had authority. But some were significant enough to warrant investigations. Although these events were mostly isolated, their occurrence often caused unprecedented procedures to be initiated. The confrontations between PCMFs and Iraqis were sometimes an altogether different matter. Some, as we will see, had consequences far beyond the geographical landscape of Iraq.

The strategic consequences of these confrontations underlie perhaps a more—in international context—significant issue. The relative impunity with which PCMFs operate is indicative of their status as a non-state actor, a role that has been growing in influence since the end of the Cold War. OIF would test this influence as it would place a non-state actor in direct confrontation with an emerging nation-state. The results of this confrontation may very well have set precedents that the United States may regret. Only time will tell. But, if it is true as some, like Christopher Spearin, have indicated,[101] that the nation-state model is losing its dominance, then we can expect that non-state actors, e.g., PCMFs, will grow even more influential. The importance of this consideration cannot be overemphasized because it implies the absolute necessity of legal reforms regarding PCMFs.

1.   Contractors and Fallujah

In March of 2004, four Blackwater contractors operating two separate SUVs led three flatbed trucks into the heart of Fallujah. At the time, Fallujah was becoming a hotbed of insurgent activity and was operating under ad-hoc, tribal structures. The First Marine Expeditionary Force (I MEF) had recently taken over military authority in the

---

[101] Christopher Spearin, *Privatized Peace? Assessing the interplay between states, humanitarians and private security companies*, as taken from *Private Military and Security Companies, Ethics policies and civil-military relations*, eds, Andrew Alexandra, Deane-Peter Baker, and Marina Caparini (NY: Routledge Press, 2008), 203–213. Spearin addresses the argument that the traditional nature of statecraft is in question. Summarizing that:

> [D]espite the emphasis placed on them in international affairs, many states in the post-colonial or post-communist contexts lack the ability to provide for their citizenries and to ensure their security as assumed in the Hobbesian bargain. The advent of human security, therefore, points towards readjusting the balance between ends and means such that individuals are threated more as the former and states as the latter. 205.

region from the 82nd Airborne Division and was intent on doing things a little bit differently. The Marines wanted more emphasis placed on engaging insurgents, but this was becoming easier said than done, as insurgent activity seemed to correspond with that of the Marines. The Marines had yet begun to advance heavily into the heart of the city, however, and were at the time conducting continuous operations in Fallujah's outskirts. With no sizeable military presence, the four Blackwater contractors were about to go directly into the city's center and, unfortunately, would not return. The Blackwater convoy was ambushed, all four contractors were killed, and their bodies were dismembered, burned, and hung from a bridge over the Euphrates. The images were startling and galvanizing.

The incident was tragic but underscored serious operational concerns. There were, of course, calls for justice and retaliation—a plea to the moral code of warriors. But, although the Blackwater contractors were Americans, they were not soldiers. They were there under contract and so the moral argument seemed out of place. Perhaps if they had been soldiers there would have been a more immediate response from the Marines. But as it were, there was some confusion regarding how to react. There were questions being raised that, until now, had gone unnoticed. Why were the men allowed to enter the city? Should there have been a military escort? Who oversaw their operations? What were their Rules of Engagement (RoE)?

Over seven years later, very similar questions are still being asked, not just about that tragic incident but about America's relationship with PCMFs in general. Ironically, had these questions been asked with more authority in 2004, perhaps another polarizing tragedy would not have happened a mere three years later. But this incident would go well beyond operational flaws. It would have strategic implications and test the very fabric of U.S./Iraq relations.

2.   Blackwater and Nisour Square

Iraq continued to present significant hurdles to all U.S. forces and officials involved, and by 2007 the situation was becoming very politically sensitive. The surge had seen thousands more of U.S. troops pour into the region in the hopes that Iraq would not devolve into a Civil War. Ethnic and tribal tensions were high, and the fledgling government was trying to assert its authority but still facing questions of legitimacy and doubt from its own constituents. In the fall of 2007, these doubts would be put to the test.

On September 16, 2007, a convoy of armored SUVs carrying Blackwater contractors and U.S. VIPs made its way into Nisour Square, Baghdad, Iraq. There are still conflicting reports over exactly what happened that day, but for whatever reason(s), the Blackwater convoy opened fire in the square. After it was over, 17 Iraqi civilians lay dead, many more wounded, and dozens of civilian vehicles destroyed or burning.[102] Blackwater claimed that their men were returning fire from insurgents while the Iraqis claimed that the shooting was unprovoked. Several members of Blackwater eventually stood trial in a U.S. District Court for their part in the shooting but the case was dismissed in 2009.[103]

The incident had an even greater impact however, than the immediate and tragic loss of lives. The shooting sparked outrage in the Arab world, polarized the opinions of the American public, and revealed publically, the growing dependence that the U.S. had upon PCMFs. The case also revealed the dramatic amount of legal latitude that surrounded PMCFs and brought into question the legality of their use. Furthermore, the incident would test, in earnest, the relationship between the U.S. and the newly formed Iraqi government. The Iraqi government demanded that Blackwater be expelled from the country and the guards tried under Sharia law. The U.S. claimed jurisdiction and stressed the valued commodities that the corporation had provided over significant operations and personnel. In perhaps a gesture to placate Arab-U.S. tension, the U.S. chose not to renew Blackwater's contract in Iraq, and therefore, effectively removed them from Iraqi soil. The blowback upon the company's image was so severe that it never fully recovered.[104]

---

[102] Jeremy Scahill's book. *Blackwater*, offers a detailed look into the Nisour tragedy including the events leading up to, during, and after the shootings.

[103] United States v. Slough, 677 F. Supp. 2d 112, 115-116 (D. C C. 2009). The court determined that the Blackwater defendants had been compelled to make self-incriminating statements regarding their actions which ultimately, threatened the viability of the prosecution. The court dismissed the case against all defendants.

[104] Blackwater tried to remodel itself after Nisour, purging many senior executives and going so far as to change its name to *Xe* (since renamed to *Academi*).

Since that fateful day, the U.S. has taken measures to regulate the use of private security with greater fidelity, but are these measures adequate? Better yet, are they even applicable?

Conclusion

At this point in the thesis the original hypothesis seems not only valid, but justified, i.e., that establishing a status-based, legal framework will promote legitimacy, increase effectiveness, and mitigate concerns—both domestically and abroad. By utilizing OIF as a case study, this chapter presented evidence of the United States' reliance on PCMFs, the depth to which this dependency runs—from manpower, to services rendered, and to budget allocation—and the consequences that this intrinsic relationship has had.

PCMFs are very real, and ultimately, can be beneficial entities in supporting U.S. force projection and operations of national interests.[105] But they cannot be incorporated effectively, i.e., without global skepticism. If realistic reforms are not taken to maximize their potential, protect all parties involved, and ensure clear means of accountability— they will continue to be a source of political tension. Therefore, PCMFs must be transparent in their actions and intent.

The following chapter will look at the peculiar omission of PCMF recognition in any formal form—besides their *post-facto* analysis. Additionally, the following chapter will take a cursory look at how the relationship between PCMFs and the United States may be unintentionally redefining a much larger field, i.e., U.S. civil-military relations (CMR).

---

[105] I am referring here to the ever growing scope of opportunities that are presenting themselves to PCMFs, i.e., peacekeeping operations, humanitarian/disaster relief operations, and of course, the wide spectrum of contingency operations – an area that, through OIF and OEF, has made them a valuable commodity on the international market.

THIS PAGE INTENTIONALLY LEFT BLANK

V. RECOGNITION VS. EFFECTIVE DEMOCRATIC CONTROL

If a strategy does not address ends, ways, and means, it is not a strategy but a set of aspirations.[106]

In traditional theory,[107] states oversee the control and application of violence. This is the recognized order of the modern world and is found in Max Weber's discourse—often the foundation for state-centric scholarly discussion. Deborah Avant cites as much, summarizing Weber's contribution as "the obvious starting point in most investigations and even those who argue that globalization and the rise of non-state actors have affected vast portions of the world's political arena generally assume that coercive power still resides with the state."[108] The rise of PCMFs has disrupted this order, however, so much so that their influence may have irreversibly damaged the states' claim as the sole proprietor of violence. As we have seen in OIF, the reliance on PCMFs was extraordinary, in some instances accounting for 50 percent of the DoD's workforce in Iraq.

While privatizing elements of force enhancement is not unprecedented, the measure to which it was done so in Iraq, was. The fact of the matter is that PCMFs now perform many of the services which, not so long ago, were considered core responsibilities of the military. Also, the nature of conflict itself has changed with contingency operations often replacing the traditional warcraft between named belligerents. In this regard, PCMFs offer attractive methods to engage and/or protect a state's interests without mobilizing its military. This is even more attractive to emerging democracies who can utilize PCMFs as a cost effective method to assert their authority, and ironically, potentially demonstrate legitimacy as a body politic capable of projecting

---

[106] Jim Lacey, "The Death of Military Strategy," online article accessed through *The National Review*, http://www.nationalreview.com/articles/271678/death-military-strategy-jim-lacey#. Jim Lacey is professor of strategic studies at the Marine Corps War College.

[107] I am referring here to prominent Political Science and Sociological thought professed by Peter Fever, Max Weber, Sam Huntington, Morris Janowitz, *et al*, wherein states are defined, at least, subjectively by the ability to wage war.

[108] Avant, *The Market of Force*, From Max Weber: *Essays in Sociology* (New York: Oxford University Press, 1946), 3.

forces on behalf of their own national interests. Furthermore, transnational actors such as NGOs and multi-national corporations are increasingly looking to PCMFs as a viable option to accomplish their goals. All of this is relevant to the position of the Westphalian state, since "a burgeoning transnational market for force now exists alongside the system of states and state forces."[109]

"Why," Avant writes, "should we worry—or even care—about this market? The answer is simple, [PCMFs] may affect how and whether people can control violence."[110] Although Avant is basing her work on MSDFs, this thesis advances that the *entire* private military industry influences the management of violence and therefore—although agreeing with her conclusion—suggests the topic be discussed more broadly. That being said, if we hold Avant's conclusion to be accurate then we immediately see the necessity for constructing the argument of this thesis. Namely, to establish control measures that will mitigate domestic and international concerns over the utilization of PCMFs in support of a democratic projection of force. But to be effective, these control measures must be universal, i.e., applicable to both states and non-state actors.

In *A History of Warfare*, John Keegan challenges the Clausewitzian theory that "war is the continuation of politics by other means." Keegan makes the assumption that Clausewitz was describing what war *ought* to be,[111] i.e., that war was waged on behalf of the state's public sphere—described by Avant as "the institution through which the use of violence could be most effectively linked to endeavors endorsed by a collective."[112] Clausewitz's theory has endured because it represents the traditional (and familiar) linkage between the use of violence for political processes and the social norms within a territory.[113] But Clausewitz could not have predicted the amount of influence of the private sphere, i.e., the mass proliferation of PCMFs and their ability to be utilized as combat multipliers or even sole, force providers to both states and transnational actors. Additionally, it is hard to imagine that Clausewitz could have foreseen the current threat

---

[109] Avant, *The Market for Force*, 3.

[110] Ibid.

[111] John Keegan, *A History of Warfare* (New York: Knopf, 1993), 1–6.

[112] Avant, *The Market for Force*, 3.

[113] Ibid.

environment; much less the impacts that COIN would have on how states—specifically Western powers—and non-state actors navigate within it.

All of this implies that the lines between national security and global security are becoming increasingly blurred.[114] Further obscuring any clarity are the interests of the non-state actors whose endeavors rarely have any collective cohesion. "This," Avant writes, "is true for moralists who feel responsible to intervene in order to help quell violence, pragmatists who worry about economic disruptions, and…realists who worry about breeding grounds for terrorists."[115] The latter comment carries significant weight, post-9/11, as the United States, as the unipolar power of the world, has taken direct interests in far-flung regions of the world under the rationale of its national security. Unable (politically and economically) to project its military into these areas in any substantial numbers, the U.S. has increasingly turned to PCMFs. Following the U.S.'s lead, various NGOs and multi-national corporations have done the same, finding the value in pursuing their own goals while remaining politically distant from potential repercussions.

Access to PCMFs have changed the landscape of violence management and greatly increased the ways and methods that any interested party can advance its own agenda beyond traditional means, i.e., uniformed force projection. This does not mean that the role of the state has been weakened—only changed to incorporate a much wider spectrum of actors and interests. The complexity of this design, however, requires significant oversight or else it runs the risk of damaging the international norms of accepted state behavior. This is even more important considering the varying capacities of states. Developed, Western powers have a substantial foundation and numerous institutions in place capable for securing the limitations of PCMF influence. Whether they are effectively utilizing them is another matter. Several emerging democratic powers however, are still struggling with the management of statecraft. Considering this, it is essential that the United States—as the democratic world leader—enact measures that will set the necessary precedents for legitimate PCMF utilization.

---

[114] Avant, *The Market for Force*, 33.

[115] Ibid., 33–34.

This chapter will look to the peculiarity of PCMF omission from the majority of the United States' security documents in order to emphasize that effective reforms cannot take place until a public admission and nationally inclusive strategy regarding PCMF capabilities is developed. This chapter will also call the government to task by highlighting its current *nom de guerre* "whole of government" approach as wholly inaccurate without the formal inclusion of PCMFs. Finally, this chapter will advance the trinity of democratic civilian control[116] offered by Professor Thomas Bruneau as the theoretical framework for future PCMF reforms.

A.   U.S. STRATEGIC TRINITY VS. THE QDR: A PECULIAR RELATIONSHIP

The reliance on PCMFs by the U.S. is understood but what about the stigma that accompanies them? Whether under the misnomer of mercenary or under the accusation that they act with questionable motives, PCMFs operate in a politically delicate landscape. For this reason, politicians, cabinet members, and senior DoS and DoD personnel want to distance themselves from any direct association with their use. Perhaps there is no better example of this than the glaring omission—at least directly—of PCMFs, the PMI, or even the term contractor in the triad of America's strategic documents.[117] Substantiating this claim is that the term contractor is mentioned directly within the 2010 Quadrennial Defense Review (QDR),[118] implying that PCMF use is recognized but only after the fact, i.e., when their utilization—especially on such a large scale as it was in OIF—cannot escape public scrutiny. Furthermore, the QDR represents

---

[116] I am referring to the three dimensions of democratic civil-military relations developed by Dr. Thomas C. Bruneau, Distinguished Professor of National Security Affairs at the Naval Postgraduate School in Monterey, California. These are: civilian authority, effectiveness, and efficiency. See, Bruneau, *Patriots for Profit*, and *Who Guards the Guardians and How*?

[117] The National Security Strategy, The National Defense Strategy, and the National Military Strategy.

[118] Jeffrey D. Brake, Quadrennial Defense Review (QDR): *Background, Process, and Issues*, Library of Congress, Washington, DC, Congressional Research Office. The congressionally mandated Quadrennial Defense Review (QDR) directs DoD to undertake a wide-ranging review of strategy, programs, and resources. Specifically, the QDR is expected to delineate a national defense strategy consistent with the most recent National Security Strategy by defining force structure, modernization plans, and a budget plan allowing the military to successfully execute the full range of missions within that strategy. The report will include an evaluation by the Secretary of Defense and Chairman of the Joint Chiefs of Staff of the military's ability to successfully execute its missions at a low-to-moderate level of risk within the forecast budget plan. Accessed through: http://www.stormingmedia.us/90/9037/A903774.html.

the entire Department of Defense as opposed to any single, staff entity or office, and is generated from within the Pentagon—the single largest governmental employer of private military and security contractors.

Perhaps, it is reasonable to surmise that the proclamations of the aggregate do not suffer the same scrutiny of the individual, and so the QDR, representing the entire DoD, has more latitude than would say, the National Defense Strategy (NDS) which represents the Secretary of Defense (SECDEF). Although a plausible assumption it has a glaring weakness—the NDS is a *strategy*, worse, it is part of *the strategy* for preserving the national security of the United States. A similar scenario could be applied to the National Military Strategy (NMS). Like the NDS, the NMS represents both the DoD and a specific office, in this case, the office of the Chairman of the Joint Chiefs of Staff (CJCS). Both documents are part of a larger scheme—formally proclaiming the national interests of the United States—but have the fallibility of being tied an individual. This means that the wording in the respective documents is purposefully ambiguous. If this contention is even closely accurate than it stands to reason that the pinnacle of the three documents—the National Security Strategy (NSS)—would perhaps be even more so as it comes directly from the Office of the President of the United States (POTUS). This is not to say that ambiguous word choice is a calamity however, as the context of a senior political document, by most accounts, should provide the issuer with a certain degree of separation. But it is to say that, as a collective strategy, the documents should reaffirm their intentions to their respective audience. At the very least, the documents should take a hard look at the ends (what do you want done?), ways (how do you want it done?), and means (what resources are available to do it with?) that it is dispensing. After all, if effective guidance is not issued during the strategy then accountability after the execution is virtually impossible.

An omission or inclusion of any specific entity by one of the documents usually correlates to the same in the other two. This is altogether fitting as it demonstrates unity of effort towards achieving U.S. objectives. But by omitting such a vital part of how the U.S. actually performs these objectives, i.e., PCMFs, the documents are revealing the same unfortunate affliction that permeates the discussion of COIN. Namely, that the documents are saying *something* without saying *anything*. The U.S. produces its strategic documents in direct relation to one another and in so doing, attempts to achieve a synergy of intentions with each document owing its legitimacy to its predecessor. For example, last year the Department of Defense released the 2011 National Military Strategy (NMS), which purports to explain how the military will support the National Defense Strategy, which in turn explains how the Department of Defense will support the objectives of the National Security Strategy. Taken together, the three documents are supposed to provide our military leaders with all the strategic-planning guidance they require for the next year.[119]

The failure of the three documents to directly mention PCMFs[120] implies that they are not a legitimate means of reaching strategic intent. Realistically, nothing could be farther from the truth. Removing direct attribution from the documents reveals a different story—as is the case in the 2010 QDR which, representing the entire DoD, has the latitude to admit the following:

> The Department is facing mission requirements of increasing scope, variety, and complexity. To ensure the availability of needed talent to meet future demands, we are conducting a deliberate assessment of current and future workforce requirements. This effort will ensure that the Department has the right workforce size and mix (military/civilian/contractor) with the right competencies. This assessment will be enterprise-wide, enabling the Department to better recruit and retain personnel with the most-needed skills.

> The services provided by contractors will continue to be valued as parts of a balanced approach that properly considers both mission requirements and overall return. In keeping with the Administration's goal of reducing the government's dependence on contractors, the Department introduced its in-sourcing initiative in the FY 2010 budget. Over the next five years,

---

[119] Lacey, *The Death of Military Strategy*, 1.

[120] It should be noted however that all three documents refer to the "private sector" and, in the case of the NSS, mentions " credibly underwriting U.S. defense commitments with tailored approaches to deterrence and ensuring the U.S. military continues to have the necessary capabilities across all domains— land, air, sea, space, and cyber. It also includes helping our allies and partners build capacity to fulfill their responsibilities to contribute to regional and global security. While the use of force is sometimes necessary, we will exhaust other options before war whenever we can, and carefully weigh the costs and risks of action against the costs and risks of inaction". *National Security Strategy*, 22. Furthermore, the NDS mentions the "total force" in pages 17 and 19, respectively but drawing conclusions to this phrase and PCMFs is subjective, at best.

the Department will reduce the number of support service contractors to their pre-2001 level of 26 percent of the workforce (from the current level of 39 percent) and replace them, if needed, with full-time government employees. These efforts will help establish a balanced total workforce of military, government civilians, and contractor personnel that more appropriately aligns public-and private-sector functions, and results in better value for the taxpayer.[121]

The reference to contractors in the QDR represents how intrinsically tied to all levels of DoD operations they have become, even going so far as to admit that some of their services may best be supplied instead by the federal workforce.

This chapter proposes that the QDR's recognition is a positive step in recognizing PCMF influence. Doing so takes precedence in addressing the pros and cons of their continued use and encourages a hard look at their cost effectiveness, legality, and legitimacy as an effective tool in promoting U.S. national interest. Conversely, failure to admit their roles in the U.S. strategic documents, regardless of the political motives, is serving three larger causes. (1) That the regulations concerning PCMF utilization will be difficult to enact, much less reformed, if they are not publically and formally included in U.S. lexicon. (2) The omission of PCMFs is facilitating their ability to continue to operate in "shades of gray"—removed from public discourse since no attention is afforded them—officially, and ultimately, with little legal and financial impunity. (3) Failure to mention them in official U.S. strategies facilitates international apprehension of U.S. motives, especially once U.S. contracted PCMFs are encountered by a host-nation; simultaneously exacerbating informal public discussion of mercenaries, e.g., Blackwater, and suspicious governmental ties to privatized corporations, e.g., KBR.

1. Whole of Government Approach and PCMF inclusion

There is fallibility with excluding PCMFs in the U.S. strategic documents. It fails to recognize them as part of the current "whole of government" approach. This phrase has come to mean the "interagency" or "interorganizational" or whatever term may be the current flavor in trying to describe the synchronization of effort among the DoD, DoS, NGOs, et al. Instituted by the Obama administration in 2010, the whole of government

---

[121] 2010 Department of Defense, *Quadrennial Defense Review*, 55-56.

approach was meant to serve as a concept, capturing the administration's intent on unifying U.S. efforts. Secretary of State, Hillary Clinton confirmed as much when she said:

> One of our goals coming into the administration was ... to begin to make the case that defense, diplomacy and development were not separate entities, either in substance or process, but that indeed they had to be viewed as part of an integrated whole and that the whole of government then had to be enlisted in their pursuit.[122]

The whole of government approach permeates the entire National Security Strategy and is indicative of the President's call for innovation and ambition across the entire spectrum of national defense. PCMFs may be implied in this regard but the term contractor is glaringly admitted. As mentioned earlier however, this omission is more a by-product of political necessity than negligence. The 2010 NSS was the Obama Administration's first, and was built upon the lessons learned in OIF/OEF and the researched conclusions of the 2010 QDR. For this reason, more consideration should have been given to the inclusion of PCMFs. After all, waging two wars without them would have been nearly impossible, while writing the QDR without mentioning them, would have been misleading. However well intended the phrase "whole of government," it is incomplete without directly admitting the role of the contractor and/or the services these entities provide.

Additionally, the admission of contractor importance to U.S. operations within the latest QDR should have encouraged a similar address in the NSS. Especially considering the emphasis the QDR takes on replacing, where applicable, contracted services with federal positions—a recognition that implies PCMFs were/are consuming a considerable portion of the DoD's budget. When read independently from the QDR however, the NSS glosses over the impact that PCMFs have in current U.S. national security initiatives, only hinting at combined efforts. But when read in conjunction with the QDR, the disparity is alarming. On the one hand is the NSS (and subsequent U.S. strategic documents) which makes no direct mention of any related PCMF terms, implying that

---

[122] Secretary of State Hillary Rodham Clinton in a speech given at the Brookings Institution, May 27th 2010, accessed at http://www.state.gov/secretary/rm/2010/05/142312.htm.

their contributions are peripheral at best. While on the other hand, is the U.S. Quadrennial Defense Review which offers not only the utility of contractors but also that their utilization has become so prevalent that it is now a valid budgetary concern, so much so that the QDR implies a reexamination of the current division of labor. Therefore, it is a reasonable assumption that the exclusion of PCMF related terms within the NSS is more akin to denial than dismissiveness.

There is another possible reason for excluding any mention of terms related to PCMFs within the NSS—control. Currently, there is a tremendous amount of confusion regarding exactly who exercise authority over PCMFs and how they are held accountable for their actions.[123] This is of great concern to politicians and senior military leaders alike since without being able to clearly define ownership or identify legal parameters they are, in essence, allowing para-military organizations and lucrative big business corporations to make their own rules. A proposition that is uncomfortable to say the least but in wartime seems borderline criminal. No respectable businessman, politician, or senior military leader is willing to offer up a topic for public discussion that provides more questions than answers. It simply does not make sense—businesswise or politically. Although, admittedly, tying this reason to individual political motives may be argumentative, it nonetheless remains at least a periphery variable that, in conjunction with the other recognitions, belies the necessity for a status–based framework of regulations.

B.   CIVIL–MILITARY RELATIONS AND BRUNEAU'S TRINITY

The lack of unity in the U.S. strategic documents not only reveals a certain level of political discomfort, it also, potentially, challenges U.S. civil–military relations from unprecedented angles. This is not to imply that the disparity recognizes a "gap" in the

---

[123] There is tremendous confusion over control vs. accountability when it comes to PCMFs. Control, in traditional U.S. terms, means a multi–layered institutional system capable of personal management over the actor – either directly or indirectly. Accountability means there is no personal level of supervision beyond that of the contract between the principal and the agent. *See*, Bruneau, *Patriots for Profit*, 157–159. While legally, accurate, the latter does little to affect organizational behavior. Both terms have been applied to PCMFs but since there really are no institutional control measures over them and current accountability measures seem lacking, U.S. politicians may choose to avoid association with the entire industry.

field of CMR similar to those already identified.[124] On the contrary, the QDR, in taking the initiative in recognizing PCMF reliance, implies a concern worthy of discussion, i.e., that the current privatized sector/DoD relationship is so symbiotic that it needs to be addressed in detail, else the arrangement could drift into an inseparable entity with the potential to become a self–sustaining and self–regulating agency. Considering this proposition a "civil–military gap" would almost be a welcome occurrence. What this section is suggesting is that the disparity in the U.S. formally recognizing the roles of PCMFs goes beyond the traditional, domestic issue of a state's democratic civilian control over its military[125] and instead is entering into uncharted waters.

This is suggested in the following two claims: (1) PCMFs have become some of the most influential non–state actors in U.S. history. (2) Globalization is rapidly expanding the market for force and increasing their influence exponentially.

This section will address these two separate but linked claims and analyze how, collectively, they are straining U.S. civil–military relations beyond historically accepted norms. In order to do this effectively, this section will analyze the three dimensions of civil–military relations advanced by Professor Thomas Bruneau, Distinguished Professor at the Naval Postgraduate School. "Bruneau's trinity"[126] will serve as the framework for understanding where and how PCMFs fit within the U.S. CMR construct and, to a larger

---

[124] I am thinking here of Paul Braken, "Reconsidering Civil–Military Relations; Richard Kohn, The Erosion of Civilian Control of the Military in the United States Today, and the RAND Corporation which published a paper in 2007 titled "The Civil–Military Gap in the United States: Does It Exist, Why, and Does It Matter?" It is interesting to note the amount of scholarly attention devoted to the mythical "gap" as it seems largely irrelevant to the bigger picture, i.e., is the military and its civilian authority acting in accordance with legitimate institutions designed to protect and preserve them both and in the best interest of national interests? If the answer is yes, then any "gap" is either nonexistent or irrelevant. Braken states this succinctly in the following:

> The central role that civilian control has played in civil–military relations is understandable. But in its raw form it is a trivial problem because under nearly any conceivable set of arrangements civilian control is assured. To over–concentrate on it when it is appropriate to do so will only elevate a host of ordinary misunderstandings and differences into a high political arena where they do not belong. Moreover, it will distract attention from other important dimensions that characterize the relationship of the military to the state. 163.

[125] I am referring here to Samuel Huntington and Peter Feaver respectively, who focus on methods of control over the armed forces.

[126] This "trinity" includes democratic civilian control, effectiveness, and efficiency.

degree within a globalized society. This not only facilitates the goal of this thesis but also may foster a normative method for PCMF inclusion across the entire spectrum of civil–military relations.

Bruneau's framework presents a comparative approach that, although originally designed to be applicable to both old and new democracies,[127] seems equally fitting as a both a measurable variable towards full integration of PCMFs into U.S. CMR, and as a stand-alone analytical tool capable of determining, through its three tiered approach, the validity of a PCMF's performance potential. This claim seems substantiated considering the similarities between PCMFs and the militaries or other instruments of security within emerging democracies. Although, initially, Bruneau's framework seems most applicable to MSDFs, it is not too far of an assumption to see its universal value across all PCMFs.

Bruneau recognizes that, regardless of emerging democracies historical ties, either to authoritarian or civilian or military rule, the new regimes tend to place a greater emphasis on democratic security than national security. He writes:

> In other words, these new regimes focus on how to ensure civilian control over the armed services, which in many cases were themselves previously in control of—or even constituted—the government. Those military–dominated regimes, by contrast, had tended to preoccupy themselves with national security, particularly internal security, often to the detriment of civil society.

But what happens to the military and/or the other elements of security provision within these new democracies? Who and /or what defines their new scope and responsibilities? Absent of explicit guidance and operating within a system that is still defining itself, these militaries and their security brethren are often left to their own accord—at least within certain limits which in most cases could be considered

---

[127] Bruneau developed his approach in 1996, shortly after he began to conduct programs on and in new democracies for the Center of Civil–Military Relations (CCMR), Naval Postgraduate School, Monterey, CA. *See, Bruneau, Patriots for Profit*, 28. Professor Bruneau is working currently with Professor *Cristina Matei* in analyzing, understanding, and teaching the lessons learned by consolidated democracies to emerging countries across the globe. Their collective works have taken unprecedented steps in identifying the need for a thorough understanding of both domestic and international civil–military relations. *See, also, Bruneau*, "Contracting Out Security," *Journal of Strategic Studies* (2012). http://dx.doi.org/10.1080/01402390.2012.663254.

rudimentary control measures designed to preserve some semblance of security while deterring abuse of authority. But is such a situation so far removed from the actions of PCMFs?

Considering that PCMFs are non–state actors with still emerging boundaries, some being instituted ad hoc, then the analogy is perhaps closer than expected. Therefore, if Bruneau's theoretical framework is, as recognized, a sufficient blueprint for balanced and legitimate civil–military relations, specifically as it applies to democratic governments, then it stands to reason that the same framework could be applied to the growing niche PCMFs are creating in CMR. Incorporating PCMFs within this framework and thus, the scholarly discussions about CMR, should provide a more complete picture of the field, subsequently providing the principal (in most cases, the U.S.) with managerial guidance, while providing the agent with expected norms of behavior. Furthermore, this framework would be beneficial in assisting to define the long–term, and potentially normative, PCMF/U.S. government (USG) relationship currently lacking in today's discussions of CMR.

The three dimensions in Bruneau's model are democratic civilian control, effectiveness, and efficiency. This section will take a look at each three and their respective applicability to the world of USG/PCMF relations. It will highlight the aspirations of each dimension as well as any weaknesses towards PCMF/CMR alliance. Collectively, it is expected that this framework should be sufficient in establishing a theoretical foundation from which the status–based regulations can begin.

1.   Democratic Civilian Control

"Democratic civilian control," Bruneau writes,

comprises three aspects: civilian authority over institutional control mechanisms, normalized oversight, and the inculcation of professional norms through professional military education. Direction and guidance must be grounded in...institutions...and [there must be] a well–defined chain of authority for civilians to determine roles and missions...Finally, the inculcation of professional norms supports the first two elements through transparent policies for recruitment, education, training, promotion, and retirement.[128]

Control is the key word here as it requires a multi–layered approach, i.e., institutions that Bruneau is emphasizing. The term control however, is often incorrectly interchanged with accountability when it comes to discussions of PCMFs. But this is a misnomer and does not adequately address the fact that there is, as of yet, any substantial institution capable of directly aligning PCMF behavior with acceptable international norms. This presents two serious concerns. First, absent the recommended institutional control, PCMFs may be "writing their own checks," i.e., determining their own roles and missions without any clear "chain of authority." And second, the U.S., as the predominant employer of PCMFs, could realistically institutionalize PCMF regulations in manners that would best serve *purely* U.S. interests.

Either of these two considerations—PCMFs operating with no clear chain of authority or the U.S. establishing self–serving institutions—seem generally devoid of transparency and thus, severely degrade any attempt at producing democratic civilian control. Combined, the results are even more ambiguous and yet, ironically, seem to be the default approach in current U.S./PCMF relations, i.e., reliance and denial running virtually hand in hand. Put another way, PCMFs present a challenge on two simultaneous fronts. (1) The U.S. needs the capabilities and provisions of PCMFs — evident in OIF, but (2), when the PCMFs behave in manners unbecoming acceptable international norms, they are dismissed as U.S. representatives.[129]

Historically, this is an accepted trend. But if PCMFs are to be used as effectively and efficiently as possible, they must first fall under transparent, democratic civilian control. Perhaps the biggest hurdle to overcome, however, may be in getting the United

---

[128] Bruneau, *Patriots for Profit*, 31.

[129] Such a precedent was set after the Blackwater shootings in Nisour Square in 2007. The Nisour Square shooting ignited tremendous political concerns. The official U.S. stance, perhaps issued in an attempt to placate Iraqi demands, stated that the Blackwater guards responsible would "be tried in Iraqi court" and "under Iraqi law." *See, Scahill, Blakwater*, 12–20. Such a statement was significant as the company was operating under a U.S. (DoS) contract but realistically, had no legal teeth behind it, primarily because in 2004, Paul Bremer had issued Order 17, effectively immunizing all contractors working for the U.S. in Iraq from Iraqi prosecution. Ibid., 15.

States government to examine the possibility that democratic civilian control, in this instance, may best be served by an international body—a proposition to be analyzed further in the next chapter. This is an admittedly substantial hurdle as the U.S. has seldom, if ever, relinquished any amount of substantial sovereignty to entities outside its own scope of influence.[130]

2.   Effectiveness

There are many nuances to this second dimension of democratic CMR. After all, how *well* an entity (security force) performs its duties is often reliant on variables outside of its scope of influence. Certainly, the "whole of government" concept comes to mind here, where agencies across the entire USG are encouraged to culminate their efforts for a desired end–state. But how well these efforts are coordinated and how seamlessly the integration is between organizations is wholly a matter of perspective. Making matters even more complex is the issue of deterrence. If a state, agency, or force remains unthreatened due to its relative invulnerability—even if it is only perceived to be so, then does that mean that the elements that fostered its security are/were effective? This is difficult to evaluate because, Bruneau writes, it is "trying to quantify a negative."[131]

If security forces—in this case, PCMFs,—are to be effective in CMR they must know what is expected of them and what resources they have available, including constraints and limitations. This, again, underscores the need for institutions. Furthermore, effectiveness requires clear guidelines and strategy—something already recognized at the beginning of this chapter as completely ambiguous or, in some regards, altogether missing from PCMF discourse.

3.   Efficiency

Efficiency is similar to effectiveness and in some cases the two words are used interchangeably. But effectiveness, in the crudest terms, means getting the most out a

---

[130] I am thinking here of the U.S. refusal to sign the United Nation Convention on the Law of the Sea, U.S. reservations with the International Criminal Court, and the refusal to ratify the Kyoto Protocol, to name a few.

[131] Bruneau, *Patriots for Profit*, 32.

given input. Phrases such as, "the most bang for your buck", or "doing more with less" are synonymous with this description. "Cost–effectiveness" is a more formally applicable term and is used often in dialogue regarding DoD expenditures and or USG initiatives. But its use is more related to optimal choices within a monopoly of services provided than as a tool of measurement.[132]

Efficiency shares another similarity to effectiveness. Namely, that it cannot exist without *some* strategy. Ironically, we again see a reference to the beginning of the chapter where the lack of a clear cut PCMF strategy was presented by analyzing the disparity in the U.S.'s strategic documents. Although the lack of a national security strategy should not necessarily come as a surprise, considering most nations (especially emerging ones) are slow to produce one. After all, when a state issues its national strategy, its government immediately subjects itself to its neighbors' scrutiny. Nonetheless, a lack of formal strategy weakens democratic CMR and, makes it virtually impossible to determine efficiency.[133]

Conclusion

This chapter presented evidence that the lack of formal strategy regarding contractors is detrimental to the USG's ability to manage PCMFs. While there are measures and agencies that have been implemented or tasked to mitigate the concerns surrounding PCMF utilization—the DoD in particular has instituted, at least rhetorically, relevant guidelines[134]—these measures cannot and will not be as effective without direct attention at the highest levels. Failure of the USG to provide ends, ways, and means to

---

[132] Bruneau, *Patriots for Profit*, 32.

[133] Efficiency (or cost–effectiveness) was/is a primary reason for the creation of the PNSR.

[134] *See*, Section 862 of the National Defense Authorization Act for Fiscal Year 2008, which gives extensive guidance to the executive branch on the topic of "contractors performing private security functions in areas of combat operations"; a 2009 DoD directive "Interim final rule" that "establishes policy, assigns responsibilities and provides procedures for the regulation of the selection, accountability, training, equipping, and conduct of personnel performing private security functions under a covered contract during contingency operations"; recommendations by the Special Investigating General for Iraq Reconstruction (SIGIR), the GAO, and the Joint Chiefs' Dependence on Contractors Task Force, to name a few. *See*, also, Bruneau, *Patriots for Profit*, 159–161.

incorporate contractors within its national security strategies exacerbates the problem. Without these provisions the USG is, in essence, defining aspirations, not strategy.

Looking beyond the doctrinal shortcomings, this chapter next focused on Professor Thomas C. Bruneau's "three dimensions of democratic civil–military relations. Bruneau's trinity of democratic civilian control, effectiveness, and efficiency serve as an analytical blueprint for addressing CMR concerns from emerging democracies, as those regimes are often seeking how to define the developing roles and responsibilities for their uninitiated militaries and various security forces. This chapter concludes that Bruneau's model is equally applicable to U.S. CMR in relation to PCMF utilization.

The lack of definitive strategy coupled with Bruneau's recognition of institutional necessity presents a solid foundation for exploring extensive methods of recommended PCMF reforms.

VI. SEEKING LEGALITY—IDENTIFYING GAPS IN THE CURRENT LEGAL FRAMEWORK WHILE OFFERING RECOMMENDED REFORMS

The new threat environment has been heralded (from the right and the left) as bringing with it new forms of warfare and the merging of security with a variety of other economic and political forms. Thus, "national" security has become difficult to distinguish from international or global security and the lines between internal and external security have blurred.[135]

The U.S. is the majority stakeholder in PCMF activity; accounting for 53 percent of PCMFs.[136] This position implies a tremendous amount in responsibility both domestically and abroad. Domestically, the proliferation and reliance on PCMFs can have significant effects on the federal workforce, budgetary considerations, and overall support of DoD/DoS operations. Internationally, as the unipolar power in the world, the U.S. has an implicit, moral obligation to all democratic societies. This obligation must be tendered with even greater fidelity in a globalized world, as the actions of one (especially the most prominent) have significant influence on all. Therefore, the recommended reform measures advanced herein are based upon the best interests of the United States, universally, and will take significant steps in mitigating domestic concerns while simultaneously securing its position of international democratic prominence.

This chapter will build upon the theoretical framework advanced in Chapter V— advancing recommended measures of reform that this thesis proposes is necessary and altogether overdue. This chapter will therefore be the most legally detailed of the thesis, relying heavily on the work of Huma T. Yasin et al., in the legal field. What follows is an analytical discussion that will examine inadequacies in current theories advocating PCMF control and recommend methods and institutions that may best address them.

---

[135] Avant, *The Market for Force*, 33.

[136] Bruneau, *Patriots for Profit*, *Figure 5.4. Geographical Distribution of PSCs*, 121. While this graphic represents PSCs in particular it represents the majority share the U.S. has in privatized warfare.

A.   PCMFS—A TWENTY-FIRST CENTURY ISSUE

PCMFs are a modern–day reality. Interwoven into the fabric of modern warfare and inextricably linked to how the U.S. operates in combat and contingency operations. Their strategic impacts, operational support, and financial considerations have made their removal from DoD/DoS operations at this point is simply untenable. In fact, this thesis suggests that they are not only a real modern–day variable but a very valuable asset in the United States' ability to project/protect its national security interests. As such they should be considered a viable option in force enhancement and operational autonomy. This should not occur however, until a thorough restructuring of the legal framework surrounding their current existence and methods of inclusion are considered. Utilizing them without such a framework in place facilitates dangerous legal precedents and ushers in questionable business practices and confusing military operations.

PCMFs have become part of the American bureaucracy and are now the poster child for the military industrial complex. Ignoring their contributions is both a disservice to the private sector and a deceitful method of wishful thinking by today's leadership— civilian and military. It is time that their impacts are brought to the forefront of planning and understanding, removing them from the umbrella of outdated and inaccurate regulations and placing them squarely in twenty-first century institutional control. Failure to do so will continue to challenge both U.S. civil–military and international relations unnecessarily.

The use of twentieth century legal lexicon to define novel twenty–first century problems further compounds the inefficiency in regulating PCMFs. Indeed, globalization has complicated once straight–forward legal categories and perhaps nowhere is this more apparent and more troubling than in the realm of armed conflict.[137] Terms which used to convey status and denote privileges in times of war are no longer easily decipherable. There have been numerous treaties, conventions, and declarations dedicated to laws that govern armed conflict but these seem out of touch in modern–day warfare. Interestingly, these previous regulations imply something so obvious that rarely have people paused to

---

[137] Yasin, *Playing Catch–Up*, 436–37.

consider it.[138] Namely, it presupposes the idea that armed conflict is definable and identifiable—at least less ambiguous than quantifying peace. But, is this accurate? Modern warfare, especially the adherence to COIN, has certainly blurred the lines of war and peace. Consider that a single PCMF can be exercising private security measures while simultaneously undertaking massive reconstruction efforts. War and peace are seemingly occurring simultaneously. In this regard, PCMFs are entities requiring both the immunization from violence that war implies as well as the diplomatic and democratic oversight that humanitarian relief efforts necessitate. It is altogether fitting then that the previously constructed theories and regulations are recognized as largely inappropriate regarding PCMF applicability.

1. The Mercenary Misnomer

Mercenaries have been a part of war since war itself. So much so, that direct attention has been given to the term through The Hague Convention, The Geneva Conventions, and the United Nations (UN) Mercenary Convention.[139] In essence, mercenaries are wartime profiteers, the "harbor an open commitment to war as a professional way of life. That is, their cooperation entails a certain devotion to war itself, in that their trade benefits from its existence…mercenaries require wars, which necessarily involves casting aside a moral attitude toward war."[140]

But the conditions that define mercenaries and that are universally accepted as the legal norms—see the Conventions listed above, require that the individual or group be participating in armed conflict. This means that PCMFs are not mercenaries—in the legal sense. First, the ambiguity of modern warfare aside, PCMFs are rarely hired to be direct participants in armed conflicts and therefore are operating outside the hostilities needed as a pre–condition for identifying mercenaries. Second, a mercenary is operating for private gain which requires proof of specific intent,[141] which is virtually impossible to obtain. "Third, mercenaries cannot be nationals of a party in conflict or a resident of a

---

138 Yasin, *Playing Catch–Up*, 436–37.

139 Ibid., 427.

140 Singer, *Corporate Warriors*, 41.

141 Yasin, *Playing Catch–Up*, 427.

territory controlled by a party in conflict."[142] This would exclude all American PCMFs in OIF as they hired a significant number of local nationals to augment their own capabilities.

While similarities certainly exist between PCMFs and mercenaries in that both are non–state parties engaged for remuneration, there are many distinctions that render the term obsolete in reference to PCMFs. This is generally because war, armed conflict, combatants, and non–combatant are all legal terms which fail to encompass the violent reality of post–conflict zones.[143] "Because the current internationally accepted legal definition of mercenaries fails to encompass the amorphous structure of PCMFs, it is essential to formulate a definition that accords PCMFs a concise legal status."[144]

B.   APPLICABILITY OF TODAY'S LEGAL MEASURES AGAINST PCMF UTILIZATION—DOMESTIC OR INTERNATIONAL REGULATORY FRAMEWORK?

"Currently, no criminal or civil jurisdictional statute exists to comprehensively adjudicate PCMF activity. As a result, Congress has repeatedly amended existing legislation to bring PCMFs within a regulatory framework."[145] There are three primary foundations from which to potentially prosecute PCMF misconduct: the Special Maritime and Territorial Jurisdiction Statute (SMTJ);[146] the Military Extraterritorial Jurisdiction Act (MEJA);[147] and the Uniform Code of Military Justice (UCMJ).[148] "All three statutes suffer severe limitations in processing PCMF misconduct and fail to provide a complete judicial remedy."[149]

---

[142] Yasin, Playing Catch–Up, 427.

[143] Ibid., 426.

[144] Ibid., 427.

[145] Ibid.

[146] The Special Maritime and Territorial Jurisdiction Statute, 18 U.S.C. §7 (2006).

[147] Military Extraterritorial Jurisdiction Act of 2000, 18 U.S.C. §§ 3261–67 (2206).

[148] Uniform Code of Military Justice, 10 U.S.C. §§ 801–946 (2006).

[149] Yasin, *Playing Catch–Up*, 428.

1. Special Maritime and Territorial Jurisdiction Statute

The SMTJ was passed in 1790 to cover eight specific areas of jurisdiction.[150] It was amended in 2001 by the USA PATRIOT ACT.[151] The SMTJ in an effort to fully encompass the many variables of conflict and contingency operations now contains a catch–all phrase the extends jurisdiction to "any place or residence in a foreign state used by missions or entities of the U.S. government with respect to offenses committed by or against a national of the United States."[152] The SMTJ was used successfully only once in the PCMF context, to prosecute a CIA contractor in the beating death of an Afghanistan detainee on a military base in Afghanistan.[153] But for the most part, the SMTJ is unacceptable as an efficient prosecution vehicle. First, it requires a correlation between criminal behavior and U.S. sovereign territory on which the act occurred. This is why the SMTJ could not be used against Blackwater over the Nisour Square tragedy—the event happened outside of U.S. territory. Second, the SMTJ only covers "offenses by or against a national of the United States." Again, most PCMFs hire local nationals to augment their capabilities and so the sector of prosecutable parties is limited.

2. Military Extraterritorial Jurisdiction Act

The MEJA is also insufficient as a punitive control measure as it too has specific criteria that fail to encompass the entirety of the PMI. In essence a person can only be charged under the MEJA if they are a member of the Armed Forces, under the

---

[150] Anthony Giardino, *Using Extraterritorial Jurisdiction to Prosecute Violations of the Law of War: Looking Beyond the War Crimes Act*, 48 B.C. L. REV. 699, 715 (2007). The Special Maritime and Territorial Jurisdiction Statute of the United States defines the limits of its jurisdiction for PCMF misconduct:

(9) With respect to offenses committed by or against a national of the United States as that term is used in section 101 of the Immigration and Nationality Act—

(A) the premises of United States diplomatic, consular, military or other United States Government missions or entities in foreign States, including the buildings, parts of buildings, and land appurtenant or ancillary thereto or used for purposes of those missions or entities, irrespective of ownership; and

(B) residences in foreign States and the land appurtenant or ancillary thereto, irrespective of ownership, used for purposes of those missions or entities or used by United States personnel assigned to those missions or entities.

[151] USA PATRIOT ACT § 803.

[152] Giardino, *Extraterritorial Jurisdiction*, 715.

[153] Yasin, *Playing Catch–Up*, 428.

employment of the Armed Forces, or accompanying the Armed Forces outside the territory of the U.S. "In order to fall within the parameters of the MEJA, the following elements must be met: (1) the offense must be punishable with a sentence of more than one year; (2) the conduct must occur outside the United States."[154] Congress amended the MEJA in 2004 to include contractors employed by "any other Federal agency, or any provisional authority, to the extent such employment relates to supporting the mission of the Department of Defense overseas."[155] Nonetheless, the MEJA suffers the same territorial limitations seen in the SMTJ, i.e., that it requires the same territorial link to the United States.[156]

3.   Uniform Code of Military Justice

Lastly, the UCMJ was amended in 2006 to include prosecutional jurisdiction over "persons serving with or accompanying an armed force in…time of declared war or a contingency operation."[157] Thus, the UCMJ theoretically subjects U.S. military accompanying PCMFs to military justice, suggesting both accountability and some measure of control through the threat of punitive action in the event of misconduct. But, realistically, the UCMJ would not withstand any significant constitutional scrutiny since military law does not provide a Fifth Amendment right to indictment by a grand jury or a Sixth Amendment right to trial by jury. Furthermore the amended UCMJ does not

---

[154] Yasin, *Playing Catch–Up*, 429.

[155] 18 U.S.C. §§ 3267. Following the Nisour Square incident, the House of Representatives overwhelmingly passed a resolution that would apply the act to contractors "where the work…is carried out in an area, or in close proximity to an area (as designated by the Department of Defense), where the Armed Forces is conducting a contingency operation."

[156] It is interesting to note that the Department of Justice attempted to prosecute Blackwater in the United States District Court of the District of Columbia. While the defendants, in their Motion to Dismiss for Lack of Jurisdiction, claimed that MEJA did not include the Nisour Square incident, the defendants based their argument solely upon the definition of "supporting the mission of the Department of the Defense." *See* Memorandum of Points and Authorities in Support of Defendants' Motion to Dismiss for Lack of jurisdiction at 16, United States v. Slough, 677 F. Supp. 2d 112 (D.D.C. 2009) (No. CR-08-0360) (RMU). A much stronger argument would have been the territorial link required by the SMTJ. The Court did not address jurisdictional issues in any of its opinions. *See* United States v. Slough, 677 F. Supp. 2d 112, 115–16 (D.D.C. 2009). *See,* Yasin, *Playing Catch–Up*, 430.

[157] *See,* UCMJ, 10 U.S.C. *See, also,* Yasin, *Playing Catch–Up*, 430.

clearly define the various categories of civilians who might accompany military forces.[158] The UCMJ is therefore, unreliable as a legal mechanism to prosecute PCMFs.[159]

C.   UNDERSTANDING MODERN THEORIES OF PCMF REGULATION

In the previous section, we have seen that the current legal framework does not adequately define PCMF jurisdiction. Further complicating matters is that the attempt to apply any of the previous mechanisms as enforceable parameters against PCMF misconduct creates more confusion than clarity and can, in essence, damage (or at least question) the current civil–military relationship. This section will address the current proposals that attempt to close the legal loopholes regarding PCMF regulation. Each will be addressed in detail in order to identify the pros and cons of their potential implementation as a punitive and/or regulatory vehicle.

1.   Extension of the Term "Mercenary"

There has been some consideration to extending the definition of mercenary to include PCMFs but as previously discussed this seems altogether unreasonable, primarily because the term mercenary is tied to the phrase "armed conflict," but also because PCMFs offer so much more than just "guns for hire." Yasin writes:

> Even if the "armed conflict" requirement were eliminated, the fundamental problem in applying the existing definition of "mercenary", or even attempting to extend the definition to fit the PCMF dilemma would still exist—the PCMF, as a hybrid quasi-corporate, quasi-military organization, was not contemplated when the "mercenary" definition was formulated. As such, regulating PCMFs using an outdated, seemingly irrelevant framework (or a modification of the same) is intellectually dishonest and devoid of pragmatism. The PCMF industry provides an array of services so vast…one single term would be incapable of accurately depicting and regulating PCMFs while taking into account the many nuances within the industry. Indeed, "even the U.N. Special Rapporteur for the Regulation of Mercenaries, Emanuel Ballesteros, spent

---

[158] For example, there is no delineation between contractors and embedded journalists.

[159] Yasin, *Playing Catch–Up*, 431.

five years trying to come up with a workable definition of a 'mercenary,' and the result was unworkable and laughably vague.[160]

It is clear that the term mercenary is "woefully inadequate"[161] in describing PCMFs. Careful consideration should be given to providing them a new legal status. One that is much more applicable to their services and subsequent utilization. PCMFs are such an anomaly and yet so intrinsically tied to U.S force projection that they must have their own method of regulation. Rather than force them into pre–conceived and largely, unenforceable, legal frameworks, this thesis recommends the creation of a new one or at the very least severely reform a mechanism already in existence and tailor it to be specifically applicable to PCMFs. Yasin writes:

> It is clear that governments are increasingly outsourcing the whole gamut of military functions to PCMFs, and therefore, it is far more pragmatic to regulate and define the industries using the framework that reflects the reality as it exists now, rather than extending the definition of "mercenary" to the current debate.[162]

2.   Corporate Self-Regulation

Certain scholarly works have argued that corporate self–regulation can provide adequate measures of accountability through the implementation of strict codes of conduct which would enforce a system recognizing and quantifying human rights principles.[163] The implication with this theory is that a PCMF faced with procedural inspections, i.e., ensuring the company has measures in place to protect and preserve human rights, will naturally set its own internal framework in order to placate the system of inspection and remain operationally functional. While such a system would, theoretically, produce conditions persistent with expected norms of ethical behavior, especially pertaining to its own employees, it would not extend its coverage to

---

[160] Ibid., 464.

[161] Yasin, *Playing Catch–Up*, 464.

[162] Ibid., 464–5.

[163] James Cockayne, et al., "Beyond Market Forces: Regulating the Global Security Industry" (2009), *available at* http://www.ipinst.org/media/pdf/publications/beyond_market_forces_final.pdf.

subcontractors. Furthermore, even though PCMFs may impose such regulations upon themselves, they have shown a proclivity to circumvent the framework in order to cut costs.[164]

The Voluntary Principles on Security and Human Rights is a non–binding set of principles designed to delineate guidelines ensuring the respect of human rights by PCMFs operating in combat zones.[165] Participants include a wide range of state governments, NGOs, private companies, and those in observer status, e.g., the International Red Cross.[166] The movement is intended to be part of a larger global effort to universally preserve and protect human rights in areas of conflict, but membership is purely voluntary and as such is relatively ineffective in serving as a controlling mechanism.

Additionally, there is the PCMF non-profit trade group, International Stability Operations Assistance (ISOA), which currently boasts membership of fifty-five PCMFs.[167] ISOA provides a code of conduct to "ensure the ethical standards of its member companies operating in conflict and post-conflict environments so that they may contribute their valuable services for the benefit of international peace and human security."[168]

> Despite the fact that the [ISOA] code includes sections on transparency, ethics, and accountability[169] and provides for the dismissal of member companies if they fail to uphold the provisions of the code, the code is not a binding document with any legal weight. Furthermore, when

---

[164] *See*, Blackwater contractors in Fallujah, 2004. (Chapter III). This was an incident where a well–known PCMF deliberately chose to ignore protocol and sent four contractors into a hostile area unsupported to deliver kitchen supplies.

[165] Voluntary Principles on Security and Human Rights, http://www.voluntaryprinciples.org/principles/introduction.

[166] Yasin, 467.

[167] *See ISOA Member Companies*, International Stability Operations Assistance, http://ipoaworld.org/eng/isoamembers.html.

[168] Yasin, *Playing Catch–Up*, 467. *See, also ISOA, Standards of Conduct*, http://ipoaworld.org/eng/isoamembers.html.

[169] Valued criteria to Bruneau's three dimensions of civil–military relations.

Blackwater withdrew from IPOA following the Nisour Square incident, IPOA's ability to regulate its membership proved impotent.[170]

While a self–regulating set of principles is commendable and the efforts of organizations assisting to supervise them are laudable, they fall short of controlling/regulating PCMF behavior. Primarily due to the fact that adherence to the principles is purely voluntary and thus there is no substantial punitive recourse for deviating outside the recommended guidelines.

3.   Incorporating International Law against Corporations

The rise of the Trans–national Corporation (TNC) is unprecedented in terms of a non–state actors' influence. The TNC has even begun to enter into realms that were previously the sole domain of the state, i.e., treaty negotiations and the creation of international organizations, e.g., the International Labor Organization. Such behavior is indicative of their place in a globalized world and may point to their potential as future developers of International Law. "Furthermore, TNCs are increasingly developing binding international law norms through customary international law. *Lex Mercatoria*, or the law between private merchants, has been recognized as enforceable by both domestic courts and international tribunals."[171] Considering that international law affords TNCs rights and privileges, it could reasonably be concluded that "TNCs should be equally responsible for ensuring accountability—particularly in the realm of international human rights."[172]

In response to the rising influence of TNCs, the UN created a working group, in 1998, to evaluate and re–define working business practices regarding human rights. The results of the working group (published in 2003) were the Draft Norms on the Responsibilities of Transnational Corporations and Other Business Enterprises with Regard to Human Rights (Draft Norms).[173] The international community failed to adopt

---

[170] Yasin, 467–68. *See, also*, Scahill, *Blackwater*, 358.

[171] Yasin, *Playing Catch–Up*, 468.

[172] Ibid.

[173] *See*, United Nations, Econ. & Soc. Council, Social and Cultural Rights: Norms on the Responsibilities of Transnational Corporations and Other Business Enterprises with Regard to Human Rights, U.N. Doc.E/CN.4/Sub.2/2003/12/Rev.2 (2003).

the Draft Norms however, and so the effort, while commendable, was in vain. Ironically, it may have been the Draft Norms emphasis on TNC responsibility that doomed its international acceptance. While, recognizing that states were the primary actors in international relations, the Norms concluded that the influence of TNC was so great that they must assume substantial global responsibility in promoting human rights. In, fact the Draft Norms drew such a parallel between TNCs and nation–states that they were only separated by degrees. The states' duties to upholding human rights were considered primary while the same duties regarding TNCs were secondary.[174] The business community took exception to the Norms conclusion.

While it could be considered plausible that as TNCs continue to evolve they may indeed be capable of establishing international laws of expectable behavior it does not seem to happening any time soon. PCMFs will most likely remain proponents of such propositions, at least for the time being, since acceptance of such a prominent role in the advancement of human rights would seem to narrow their current capabilities—at least to some degree.

> While this theory of regulation for PCMFs may be possible in the future, it appears that there is no current structure that would provide such direct legal accountability on corporations. As such, there is a need to develop a body that would adequately delineate PCMF responsibility for violations of human rights and delineate what state or international body would prosecute them.[175]

### 4.	State Doctrines of Responsibility

Several legal discussions have proposed extending a state's responsibility to punish PCMF misbehavior to contracting states.[176] This is a plausible contention as "both international and domestic law has long recognized the principle that states may be subject to violations of international law even where the state has not directly committed

---

[174] Yasin, *Playing Catch–Up*, 468.

[175] Ibid., 470.

[176] *See, e.g.*, Oliver R. Jones, *Implausible Deniability: State Responsibility for the Actions of Private Military Firms*, 24 Connecticut Journal of International Law 239 (2009); Steven R. Ratner, *Corporations and Human Rights: A Theory of Legal Responsibility*, Yale Law Journal 111 (2001). *See, also*, Yasin *Playing Catch–Up*, 470–72.

the violation."[177] The UN's International Law Commission established "a set of principles which govern the responsibility of States for internationally wrongful acts"[178] These principles came to be known as the Draft Articles.

The Draft Articles are essentially divided into two parts. Part one refers to the primary rules (responsibilities) of states. Namely, that states are held directly accountable for actions inherently and universally tied to the Westphalian state, e.g., adherence to the Law of the Sea and the legitimate use of force. Part two refers to the secondary rules of the state.

> Essentially, [the] secondary rules place responsibility upon the states for acts committed by state agents. Thus, the Draft Articles create a framework within which states may be liable for illegal actions that have been committed by another entity, so long as a nexus exists between the state and the acting agent.[179]

There has been discussion advocating the rules of attribution be extended to PCMFs in combat zones and/or operating in contingency operations. This is summarized by Professor Steven Ratner, who writes: "This theory asserts that corporate duties are a function of four clusters of issues: the corporation's relationship with the government, its nexus to affected populations, the particular human right at issue, and the place of individuals violating human rights within the corporate structure."[180] Essentially, this provides two legal recourses to affect control over PCMFs by assigning liability to the state: (1) if the corporation is performing duties so inherently governmental that the corporate entity should be considered an organ of the state. (2) If the entity does not meet the latter criteria, the state may still be liable if it has total control over the corporation. With these two possibilities considered, it is reasonable to conclude that a state may be held legally liable for PCMF misconduct.[181]

---

[177] Ibid., 470.

[178] *See*, UN Law Commission, Draft Articles on State Responsibility, introduction.

[179] Yasin, *Playing Catch–Up*, 470.

[180] Ratner, *Corporations and Human Rights: A Theory of Legal Responsibility*, Yale Law Journal 111 (2001): 496–97.

[181] Yasin, *Playing Catch–Up*, 472–73.

Influencing PCMF behavior by extending punitive measures to states is, in theory, a sound contention but in practice seems unlikely. There are just too many legal loopholes and extenuating variables for this theory to withstand any substantial scrutiny and thus serve as an effective regulatory mechanism. Yasin sums this up succinctly in the following:

> While using principles of attribution based on state responsibility may provide a potential means of accountability, the theory falls short of providing comprehensive regulation of PCMFs on several levels. First, the Draft Articles are not binding and are, in fact, expressly intended to be non-binding. As such, any legal argument based upon attribution must affirmatively demonstrate that the Draft Articles have become part of customary international law. Second, the international courts that have adjudicated claims involving state liability have employed the "overall control" test, which requires a high evidentiary burden of proof. Third, there is no designated international body that monitors non-state actors, and although the International Criminal Court ("ICC") may arguably exercise jurisdiction, the United States, as the largest PCMF employer, has expressly repudiated its jurisdiction. Thus, it seems very unlikely that PCMF misconduct will be legally imputable to the employing state, and even assuming arguendo that liability were attributed, there is no enforcement mechanism, particularly in the case of the United States.[182]

5.   Contract Regulations

Currently, there is little if any transparency within the PCMF marketplace. The majority of PCMF contracts have been awarded on a no–bid basis, free from peer competition and devoid of public disclosure regarding the contracts terms. This process has severely hampered any legitimate accountability measures. To make matters worse these contracts are often sub–contracted out, complicating an already opaque system through additional layers of business agreements. The no–bid process has eliminated the open market system with the former being the predominate method of doing business in OIF. In fact, it is estimated that only $47 million was awarded to PCMFs bidding in the open market, translating to billions of dollars being awarded to PCMFs devoid of any competition an outside public scrutiny.[183] Even the Freedom of Information Act (FOIA)

---

[182] Yasin, *Playing Catch–Up*, 473.

[183] Isenberg, *Shadow Force*, 65.

fails to provide any real insight into the PCMF's contracting methods. Although, through the FOIA, PCMFs can be petitioned to produce contractual terms, the PCMF can claim "confidentiality" on behalf of the entity or person with whom they are doing business. This in effect provides PCMFs with veto authority and renders full public disclosure highly unlikely. Furthermore, although military contracts could in theory be requested, this would potentially violate the FOIA's national security clause, thus preventing release of any relevant documents.

PCMF contracts generally have two primary classifications: (1) Blanket purchase or (2) Cost–plus agreements. Blanket purchase agreements, often referred to as indefinite delivery/indefinite quantity (ID/IQ) contracts refer to a process in which the principal requests items or services as the need arises. While commonplace, the process creates an open–ended contract with uncertain parameters. Cost–plus contracts are awarded to a PCMF under the pretense that the government has agreed to a fixed fee regardless of performance. This contract virtually eliminates incentives for ensuring quality services as well as controlling costs.[184]

Some commentators have recommended an extensive reform of the contractual process, incorporating public law values in the underlying contractual agreement.[185] "Because contracts are the very instruments that facilitate the shift from the public realm (of military duties) to the private sector, it follows that the contract should codify the level of accountability to which a public actor would be subject. Thus, states could use the contract as the mechanism for eliminating the disparity between the public and private spheres, by aligning interests and accountability."[186]

While plausible as a possible controlling mechanism, contract regulation cannot stand alone. Yasin contends that there are numerous variables[187] why the contracting process may not be ample enough to strictly regulate PCMF behavior. While this seems

---

[184] Yasin, *Playing Catch–Up*, 473–74.

[185] Laura A. Dickinson, *Government for Hire: Privatizing Foreign Affairs and the Problem of Accountability Under International Law*, William & Mary Legal Review 135 (2005): 161.

[186] Yasin, *Playing Catch–Up*, 474.

[187] Yasin cites many plausible variables that affect the effectiveness of contractual regulations alone. *See*, Playing Catch–Up, 474–76.

accurate, the contracting process is nonetheless a solid foundation from which to extend a regulatory framework and, at the very least, should be considered a vital instrument in influencing PCMF behavior and subsequently, effective legal control.

6. Market Regulations

There is some relative discourse on the applicability of open–market influence affecting the accountability of PCMFs but this, as seen previously, is a relatively flawed argument as it presupposes the cost–effective benefits of market competition. As already discussed the majority of PCMFs enter into contractual obligations largely devoid of any substantial competition and so the idea of market regulation seems to hold little merit. Even after claims of fraud and abuse or tragic incidents directly involving PCMF personnel the market rarely if ever holds PCMFs accountable. A perfect example of this is the Abu Ghraib prison scandal in which CACI personnel were directly implicated for egregious behavior. The USG not only failed to cancel the standing contract, it actually extended it. "Furthermore, in March of 2010, CACI was awarded a $588 million indefinite delivery and indefinite quantity contract to support the U.S. Navy's Space and Naval Warfare Systems Command's command and control operations."[188] Outcomes such as these render the market regulation theory highly skeptical as an effective mechanism of PCMF control.

7. Extension of the Military Extraterritorial Jurisdiction Act

The MEJA was simply never intended to incorporate private security companies or contractors supporting USG endeavors in a conflict zone. It was based on a domestic case of spousal abuse in Germany.[189] It holds the same intrinsic ties to territory that the SMTJ does. Even after Congress amended the MEJA in 2004, it still lacks sufficient

---

[188] Yasin, *Playing Catch–Up*, 478.

[189] Specifically, MEJA was written after a man sexually abused his thirteen year-old daughter on a military base in Germany. The man was a civilian, and his conviction was overturned because U.S. courts lacked jurisdiction over crimes committed by civilians on U.S. bases abroad. *Id.* MEJA was established to enable "the prosecution of non-military family members on US bases by allowing investigators . . . and prosecutors to apply US criminal law outside of the territorial US." *See*, Yasin, 481.

legal authority to withstand extensive scrutiny. Peter Singer revealed the weaknesses within the MEJA through a hypothetical scenario in which a drunken contractor killed an Iraqi civilian:

> Some US attorney would have had to decide to prosecute the accused, even though the victim and accused wasn't in his district, fly out to the base in Iraq multiple times, try to track down and depose witnesses (who most likely would have been deployed all over the place to avoid him), and then sell it to a jury back in the US, likely spending his entire yearly budget on one case when he is actually being judged by his bosses on his prosecutions of a lacrosse team, gang violence, or whatever. They would decide it's a loser and most likely bury it in an "open file" somewhere. And this is if there were no political pressures, and the accused was actually in custody, which military folks haven't been putting contractors in when they know of such events.[190]

Considering the difficulties in applying the MEJA to PCMF personnel the recognition of the Act as an effective control mechanism seems virtually untenable. The MEJA could become viable, however, if sufficient international measures were taken in concert. It is possible that the MEJA could be used as a vehicle for domestic jurisdiction, but, again, not without significant changes.[191]

8.   Creation of an International Body

This chapter seconds the recommendation of Peter Singer, i.e., the creation of an international body as an autonomous governing organization to regulate PCMF behavior and facilitate firm legal regulations capable of punishing deviation from prescripted norms.[192] But it should be noted (and as mentioned in the previous chapter), that recommending such an entity is easy, seeing it to fruition, highly difficult. A public international body (PIB) would provide legitimacy to PCMF utilization greater than what currently exists, but it would require the U.S. to support an entity that, quite frankly, is not as personally invested in PCMFs as the U.S. DoD and DoS. Further, if the U.S. is

---

[190] Peter Singer, *Frequently Asked Questions on the UCMJ Change and its Applicability to Private Military Contractors*, Brookings Institute, (Jan. 17, 2007), http://www.brookings.edu/opinions/2007/0112defenseindustry_singer.aspx.

[191] Yasin, *Playing Catch–Up*, 481.

[192] Singer, *Corporate Warriors*, 241.

able to generate enough political will domestically to regulate and institutionalize PCMF behavior, why then, would they defer the authority internationally?

First, the international body would fall under the auspices of the United Nations and be comprised of regulatory experts able to effectively vet PCMFs as sanctioned businesses. Next, this body would have the "right of refusal" applying incentives for appropriate behavior ranging from following human rights protocols to proper contractual processes. When taken together these first two criteria alleviate the U.S. from assuming sole responsibility for contract management and from being held directly responsible (even if only argumentative) for PCMF behavior. Of course this presupposes that the U.S. and the PMI are willing to allow external, international reviews of the contracting process. Admittedly, this may not be financially beneficial for the PCMF but this is exactly my point. The creation of the international process institutes (and incorporates) some of the already suggested theories for reform, e.g., corporate self–regulation, state doctrines of responsibility, and contract and market regulations. In doing so, the international body shows both financial and moral promise, i.e., mitigating the cost–plus and no–bid process, while protecting states from human rights violations – or at least provide a legitimate means for punitive recourse should such an event occur.

Such an international body is the first step in achieving any tangible regulatory reforms necessary for full–fledged and legitimate PCMF inclusion. While this thesis agrees with Yasin, that PCMF regulation is an "international problem requiring an international solution."[193] This chapter recommends that such a solution cannot occur without the express interest of the United States. As such, the recommendations advanced must be tempered with the expectations of full U.S. involvement.

The establishment of the international body is central to this thesis' hypothesis that establishing a status-based, legal framework will promote legitimacy, increase effectiveness, and mitigate concerns—both domestically and abroad. Furthermore, the creation of such an organization is the underlying basis for this chapter's regulatory framework and would be the primary mechanism by which "PCMF status would be

---

[193] Yasin, *Playing Catch–Up*, 482.

explicitly designated and the corresponding legal obligations attached."[194] This chapter will conclude by combining Singer's recommendations with Yasin's extensive research.

D.   SEEKING A STATUS-BASED FRAMEWORK AND THE CREATION OF THE PIB

> Perhaps no function of government is deemed more quintessentially a 'state' function than the military protection of the state itself. Indeed, scholars of privatization in the domestic sphere have often assumed that privatization of the military is one area where privatization does not, or should not, occur.[195]

This is a significant point as PCMFs exist in a nexus of civil–military provisions. Both entities can provide services mutually exclusive of each other or in a symbiotic relationship. But whereas, the military has a strict code of enforcing its standards, e.g., the UCMJ; the PCMF has no such definitive framework. Ironically, PCMFs operate within virtually the same environment as the military yet is not subject to the same regulations. PCMFs are also growing in numbers, scope, and influence but the international community as yet has failed to recognize this fact. But ignoring the problem, regardless of how convenient, does not make it go away.

"International and domestic law must adapt to bring PCMFs within the purview of a legal framework that would accord both accountability and protection based on assigning PCMFs a definitive legal status."[196] The current legal ambiguity is neither sustainable nor pragmatic—permitting PCMFs to operate free from punitive measures, setting dangerous legal precedents in the process. "Furthermore, the absence of any legal consensus regarding PCMFs results in uncertainties and inconsistent results. For example, which states have jurisdiction to prosecute, what laws govern misconduct, and to whom—or, alternatively, to what—is the PCMF responsible?"[197]

The majority of scholarly discussions regarding PCMF regulation attempts to include them into pre–existing legal definition or body of law. But these attempts offer

---

[194] Ibid.

[195] Dickinson, *Government for Hire*: 147.

[196] Yasin, *Playing Catch–Up*, 484.

[197] Ibid.

little substantive value into rectifying the confusion. In fact, these attempts actually help demonstrate just how clouded the law of governing PCMFs has become. An intensive restructuring of the legal framework addressing PCMFs would be much more effective for all parties involved.

This chapter concurs with Yasin, in that there must first be a "comprehensive multilateral treaty that defines the status of PCMFs, delineates jurisdiction, and provides for mandatory domestic enforcement in response to any violations of the treaty norms that occur."[198] This is in direct support of the public international body (PIB) proposed by Singer.[199] Singer's PIB would be led by a task force that includes virtually all stakeholders with interests in PCMF utilization. These would be, but not limited to, the following: "state actors, human rights NGOs, PCMFs themselves, and experts on international human rights law and humanitarian law."[200] Yasin further defines Singer's PIB by assigning four primary responsibilities to the task force. In no certain order:

> the task force would be responsible for: (1) creating status–based categories defining the type of PCMF;[201] (2) determining codes of acceptable conduct, accountability, and protection relative to ascribed status; (3) registering, auditing, and providing ongoing oversight of PCMF activities; and (4) providing a mandatory requirement for contracting states to prosecute PCMFs in cases of misconduct.[202]

The PIB would require corporations to register as PCMFs, cementing the vetting process within a disinterested third–party. This registration provides would provide the global community with an ample pool of potential suppliers of various force related provisions. Further, the registration process would facilitate assigning the registering corporation into one of the six classifications seen in Chapter I. This classification would also assist in assigning the PCMF a set of conditions, expectations, and legal guidelines

---

[198] Yasin, *Playing Catch–Up*, 485.

[199] Peter Singer, *War, Profits, and the Vacuum of Law: Privatized Military Firms and International Law,* Columbia Journal of Transnational Law 42 (2004): 545–46.

[200] Yasin, 486. Full inclusiveness is strongly desired here so as to impart fairness, checks and balances, and transparency among all parties.

[201] Definition and classification of PCMFs was identified as critical in the beginning of this thesis. *See*, Chapters I & II. The process of identifying them into six categories seems further substantiated by the creation of the PIB – an entity capable of effectively vetting and monitoring the entire PMI.

[202] Yasin, 486.

in direct proportion to their potential exposure to hostilities. Failure of a PCMF to register with the PIB removes them from the list of legitimate considerations for force provision and with it; the potential legal protection awarded its employees and hiring agent(s). Additionally, the PIB would theoretically, serve as an additional layer of protection regarding humanitarian issues, ensuring that registered PCMFs are in accordance with international accepted human rights norms. This should be an altogether desirable condition for the PCMF as it insulates them, to a degree, from human rights violations. The PIB would be an international mediator between the PCMF and the hiring principal and would ensure proper protocol regarding contractual obligations as well as serve as a guarantor of PCMF capabilities—ensuring that the "PCMF is in fact capable of performing services offered effectively."[203] Finally, the PIB's involvement would "provide transparency and serve to effectively eradicate no–bid, GSA, or illicit contracts, and will provide oversight to dubious sub–contracts."[204]

While the existence of rogue refusals to participate in the PIB or accept its suggestions is certainly a possibility, "states stand to benefit considerably from the enactment of such an international body."[205] The PIB would provide consistency to an inconsistent market, classifying corporations with assurance of services. This provides states with a guarantee that they are contracting a legitimate corporation for legitimate ends. Yasin writes:

> As such, states may contract freely with registered PCMFs without risking liability under doctrines of state responsibility. This relieves states of the significant onus of continued oversight and regulation over companies. The value of this effect cannot be overstated—if states are outsourcing primarily for market efficiencies, but have to perform an ongoing regulatory function, the value of this efficiency decreases substantially.[206]

---

[203] Yasin, *Playing Catch–Up*, 491.

[204] Ibid.

[205] Ibid., 494.

[206] Ibid.

Conclusion

While the creation of the PIB is critical to establishing any substantial status–based regulations and facilitating the necessary reforms required for efficient PCMF utilization, so too are the precedents of the United States, specifically as they relate to the code of law regarding PCMF utilization. Failure to adopt more stringent methods of control over PCMF behavior, and the contracting process as a whole, will continue to exacerbate an already tumultuous situation. As suggested throughout this work, if the U.S. does not fully recognize formally and publicly the reliance it has placed on PCMFs, then encouraging reformation from the international community will seem hypocritical at best. For the multilateral treaty defining PCMFs and the PIB to be effective it must be embraced first by the U.S. Congress must consider adopting statutes incorporating the treaty's provisions into domestic law. Further, rather than continuing to amend inapplicable measures, e.g., the MEJA, Congress should consider creating a statute specifically for PCMFs providing the PMI ample notice for potential prosecutions.[207] Finally, "Congress should pass a criminal and civil jurisdictional vehicle to comprehensibly cover all PCMF behavior where the United States is the contracting state or where the PCMF is a registered corporation in the United States."[208] Such measures, while admittedly bold, should garner strong international support[209] and would almost guarantee a complete restructuring of the legal framework surrounding PCMF utilization.

---

[207] Yasin, *Playing Catch–Up*, 493.

[208] Ibid.

[209] Theoretically, these precedents should generate significant traction within the UN towards the creation of the PIB.

Domestically, these measures would bring PCMFs under the collective fold of U.S. civil military relations, taking great strides towards democratic civilian control, effectiveness, and efficiency.[210]

---

[210] BARACKOBAMA.COM, http://www.barackobama.com/pdf/Defense_Fact_Sheet_FINAL.pdf. In 2007, Obama stated, "We cannot win a fight for hearts and minds when we outsource critical missions to unaccountable contractors. To add insult to injury, these contractors are charging taxpayers up to nine times more to do the same jobs as soldiers, a disparity that damages troop morale." Also, acknowledging the rampant cavalier cowboy or renegade attitude that pervaded the PCMF industry, Obama stated, "Most contractors act as if the law doesn't apply to them. Under my plan, if contractors break the law, they will be prosecuted." However, none of the proposed changes have been initiated since President Obama has taken office. Furthermore, defense spending on PCMFs has only continued to escalate under this administration, illustrating the need to rely on supranational authority to inform the limits of PCMF use. *See* Nick Baumann, *Barney Frank to Obama: Cut Military Spending*, MOTHER JONES, http://motherjones.com/politics/2009/02/barney-frank-obama-cut-military-spending.

VII. SUMMARY AND FINAL THOUGHTS

Chapter I introduced us to the term Privately Contracted Military Firm (PCMF) and provided a brief, macro view of the Private Military Industry (PMI)

Chapter II discussed the rise of the PMI as a whole, the subsequent proliferation of PCMFs, and assigned them to six discernible classifications. While the history of the PCMF is of course necessary it is the classification with which the majority of attention should be given as these classifications become essential to the author's recommendations.

Chapter III suggested that the Vietnam War may have set the conditions for future U.S. reliance on PCMFs. This chapter does not intend to counter conventional theory—that PCMFs began to materialize as we know them post–Cold War. On the contrary, this chapter means to compliment that theory, but extends the discussion to include the Vietnam era due to the highly unethical business and political decisions that seemed to surround that particular war. While of course controversial, it is not unreasonable to believe similar business/political practices are facilitating PCMF influence today. This chapter also takes a critical look at how the U.S. military's reliance on COIN—a theory rooted in Vietnam—may be exacerbating PCMF reliance.

Chapter IV focused on PCMF utilization in OIF and OEF but the preponderance of information centered on the Iraq Theater of War. There were two primary reasons for this: (1) the author has extensive experience with and first–hand knowledge of PCMFs in Iraq; and (2) there is substantial information coming out from OIF now that the war has all but ended—albeit, from a purely military standpoint. This chapter also identified a potentially tremendous benefit that PCMFs provide—mainly that their existence and subsequent utilization on the battlefield alleviates the U.S. military from deploying more troops than currently witnessed.

Chapter V was comprised of two distinct parts. Part one, focused on the tremendous disparity in America's strategic documents regarding the inclusion of PCMFs. This peculiarity highlights a larger point, that until the U.S. adopts more meaningful language and directly accepts responsibility for its reliance on PCMFs, the ambiguity of PCMF legality will continue, making any substantial reform measures highly difficult. Furthermore, without U.S. agreement to such, the international community will continue to remain morally detached from enforcing PCMF accountability.

Part two, addressed the three dimensions of civil–military relations as defined by Professor Thomas C. Bruneau. The" trinity" of democratic civilian control, effectiveness, and efficiency are presented as a theoretical foundation to designing a status–based framework capable of effectively governing the new entity within CMR—the PCMF.

This chapter also recognized the difficulty in establishing democratic control over PCMFs from an international standpoint – introduced in this chapter for future consideration as a possible (and significant) reform measure.

Finally, Chapter VI concludes with the extensive legal recommendations for PCMF regulatory reform. This chapter draws heavily from the extensive research performed by Huma Yasin as well as the ideas advanced by one of the foremost experts on PCMFs—Peter Singer. Combining the efforts of both, respectively, with the theoretical provisions provided by Thomas Bruneau, this chapter presents an international body capable of governing the discernible classifications of PCMFs effectively, efficiently, and under the auspices of democratic civilian control.

This thesis concludes that PCMFs are a valuable addition to twenty-first century warfare. Their contributions cannot be ignored. But so many stigmas seem to follow their use that ignoring them almost seems the best possible course of action. This thesis contends that is exactly what should *not* be done. Three overall areas were covered that support this recommendation. First, the cost-effectiveness of utilizing PCMFs is questionable but this thesis argues that these costs can be mitigated through extensive reform measures. Further, these reforms may prove beneficial across the entire spectrum of COIN as the actions of those supporting the force can be just as significant as the forces themselves. Failure to fully grasp the operational environment by *all* parties can cause duplicity of effort and exhaust valuable resources unnecessarily. Second, the sheer number of contracted personnel cannot be discounted. In OIF alone, some one hundred and eighty thousand contractors supported DoD/DoS endeavors. Absent reinstituting a draft, these numbers are virtually irreplaceable. Although public concerns may center on the financial expenditures of the USG towards PCMF employment, it is hard to believe these concerns would retain their integrity if talk of a reinstituting the draft became prevalent. Last, the errant behavior patterns exhibited by a select few PCMFs are not indicative of the entities themselves as much as of the system which cannot adequately enforce human rights standards and ethical norms. Although it is theoretically possible that the U.S. could resolve these issues domestically, I do not believe that such a resolution would be nearly as effective as it could be should it be created internationally. Creating a PIB similar in scope to both Singer's and Yasin's conclusions would not only be more effective, it would also be more efficient—alleviating the burden of responsibility, not sovereignty, from the U.S. Such an endeavor would require substantial political will but I believe that if the U.S. were to lead this charge the government would be in position to influence the outcome—something that has proven historically accurate and advantageous—both to U.S. national security interests and to the expansion of global norms of democratic civilian control. Perhaps, best summed up by Professor Bruneau, who writes:

> Until Congress and the White House are ready to acknowledge that this is an issue critical to the country's defense and security, until the Department of Defense is able to change the way it does business, and until lawmakers can pass, and enforce implementation of, the needed legislation, we are likely to continue dealing with confusion, ineffectiveness, and inefficiency of private [military] contracting as it is today.[211]

---

[211] Bruneau, *Patriots for Profit*, 163.

THIS PAGE INTENTIONALLY LEFT BLANK

LIST OF REFERENCES

Alabarda, Yusuf and Rafal Lisowiec. "The Private Military Firms—Historical Evolution and Industry Analysis." Master's thesis. Naval Postgraduate School, 2007.

Anderson, David. *The Vietnam War. Twentieth Century Wars.* Basingstoke, UK: Palgrave Macmillan Press, 2005.

———. *Trapped by Success: The Eisenhower Administration and Vietnam 1953–1961.* New York: Columbia University Press, 1991.

Avant, Deborah D. *The Market for Force, The Consequences of Privatizing Security.* New York: Cambridge University Press, 2007.

Blizzard, Stephen M. "Increasing Reliance on Contractors on the Battlefield; How Do We Keep From Crossing the Line?" Air Force Journal of Logistics vol. no. XXVIII (2004): 2–13. Accessed at http://www.aflma.hq.af.mil/shared/media/document/AFD-100120-044.pdf.

Brake, Jeffrey D. Quadrennial Defense Review (QDR): *Background, Process, and Issues, Library of Congress.* Washington, DC: Congressional Research Office.

Bracken, Paul. "Reconsidering Civil–Military Relations," in Don Snider and Miranda A. Carlton–Carew, ed., *U.S. Civil–Military Relations in Crisis or Transition?* Washington, DC: Center for Strategic and International Studies, 1995: 145–63.

Briody, Dan. *The Halliburton Agenda. The Politics of Oil and Money.* New Jersey: John Wiley and Sons, Inc., 2004.

Bruneau, Thomas C. "Contracting Out Security." *Journal of Strategic Studies* (2012). http://dx.doi.org/10.1080/01402390.2012.663254.

———. *Patriots for Profit.* Stanford, CA: Stanford University Press, 2011.

Bruneau, Thomas C. and Scott D. Tollefson, eds. *Who Guards the Guardians and How? Democratic Civil-Military Relations.* Austin: University of Texas Press, 2007.

Bruneau, Thomas C. and Steven Boraz. "Intelligence Reform: Balancing Democracy and Effectiveness." *Reforming Intelligence: Obstacles to Democratic Control and Effectiveness.* Austin: University of Texas Press, 2007.

Business Week. "Vietnam: How Business Fights the War on Contract." March 5, 1965. Online library resources accessed at http://www.virtual.vietnam.ttu.edu.

CACI. "23 War Profiteers' News" (April, 14, 2010). http://www.wri-irg.org/node/9927.

Carmola, Kateri. "Private Security Contractors and New Wars." *Risk, Law and Ethics* 11 (2010).

Caro, Robert A. *Means of Ascent. The Years of Lyndon Johnson*. New York: Random House, 1990.

Commission for Wartime Contracting. "Final Report on U.S. Contracting in Iraq. 2003-2011." http://www.wartimecontracting.gov/.

Clausewitz, Carl von. *On War,* edited and translated by Michael Howard and Peter Paret, introductory essays by Peter Paret, Michael Howard, and Bernard Brodie, Rev. ed. Princeton, N.J. : Princeton University Press, 1984, c1976.

Cockayne, James ed. Alison Gurin, Emily Speers Mears, Iveta Cherneva, Sheila Oviedo, and Dylan Yaeger. "Beyond Market Forces: Regulating the Global Security Industry" (2009). Accessed at http://www.ipinst.org/media/pdf/publications/beyond_market_forces_final.pdf.

Congressional Budget Office, *Contractors' Support of U.S. Operations in Iraq, 2010.* Accessed at http://www.cbo.gov/sites/default/files/cbofiles/ftpdocs/96xx/doc9688/08-12-iraqcontractors.pdf.

Department of Defense, Directorate for Information Operations and Reports. "Selected Manpower Statistics Fiscal Year 1990," AD-A235 849, Washington Headquarters Services. http://siadapp.dmdc.DoS.mil/personnel/MILITARY/history/tab9.

———. National Defense Strategy, 2008.

———. National Military Strategy, 2011.

———. Quadrennial Defense Review, QDR, 2010.S.

Dew, Nicholas, and Ira Lewis. *The Evolving Private Military Sector: Toward a Framework for Effective DoD Contracting*. Master's thesis. Presented at Naval Postgraduate School. Monterey, CA, 24 August, 2009.

Dickinson, Laura. A. "Government for Hire: Privatizing Foreign Affairs and the Problem of Accountability Under International Law." *William & Mary Legal Review* 135. (2005): 161–202.

Elliot, Mai. *RAND in Southeast Asia. A History of the Vietnam War Era*. Santa Monica, CA: RAND Co. Publishing, 2010.

Engbrecht, Shawn. *America's Covert Warriors: Inside the World of Private Military Contractors*. Dulles, VA: Potomac Books, 2011.

Epley, William W. "Contracting in War: Civilian Support of Field Armies." Army Logistician. vol. no. 22 (November/December 1990): 30–35.

Fainaru, Steve. *Big Boy Rules: America's Mercenaries Fighting in Iraq*. Philiadelphia, PA: De Capo Press, 2008.

Feaver, Peter D. *Armed Servants: Agency, Oversight, and Civil–Military Relations*. Cambridge, MA: Harvard University Press, 2003.

Frye, Ellen L. Private Military Firms in the New World Order: How Redefining "Mercenary" Can Tame the "Dogs of War." *Fordham L. Rev.* 73 (2005): 2607.

General Raymond T. Odierno. *Memorandum: Increased Employment of Iraq Citizens Through Command Contracts, Multi-National Force-Iraq*. January 31, 2009.

Giardino, Anthony. *Using Extraterritorial Jurisdiction to Prosecute Violations of the Law of War: Looking Beyond the War Crimes Act*, 48 B.C. L. REV. 699, 715. 2007.

Head, William and Lawrence E. Grinter, eds. "Vietnam and Its Wars: A Historical Overview of U.S. Involvement." *Looking Back on the Vietnam War. A 1990s Perspective on the Decisions, Combat, and Legacies*. London: Greenwood Press, 1993.

Helsing, Jeffrey W. *Johnson's War/Johnson's Great Society, The Guns and the Butter Trap*. Westport, CT: Praeger Publishers, 2000.

Herring, George C. "Johnson Administration's Limited War in Vietnam." in *Looking Back on the Vietnam War: A 1990's Perspective on the Decisions, Combat, and Legacies,* edited by William Head and Lawrence E. Grinter. London: Greenwood Press, 1993.

Hess, Gary. *South Vietnam Under Siege, 1961–1965. Kennedy, Johnson, and the Question of Escalation or Disengagement*. in *The Columbia History of the Vietnam War*, edited by David L. Anderson.. New York: Columbia University Press, 2011.

Huntington, Samuel P. *The Soldier and the State: The Theory and Politics of Civil–Military Relations*. Cambridge, MA: Belknap Press, 1981. (Originally published in 1957).

International Stability Operations Assistance. http://ipoaworld.org/eng/isoamembers.html.

Isenberg, David. *Shadow Force: Private Security Contractors in Iraq*. Praeger Security International. Westport, CT: Praeger Press, 2009.

Jones, Oliver R. "Implausible Deniability: State Responsibility for the Actions of Private Military Firms." *Connecticut Journal of International Law* 24 (2009): 221–239.

Keegan, John. *A History of Warfare*. New York: Knopf, 1993.

Kimball, Jefferey. *Nixon's Vietnam War*. Lawrence, KS: Kansas University Press, 1998.

Kohn, Richard H. "The Erosion of Civilian Control of the Military in the United States Today." *Naval War College Review*, 55 no. 3 (2008): 9–59.

Komer, Robert W. *Bureaucracy at War. U.S. Performance in the Vietnam Conflict.* Boulder, CO: Westview Press, 1986.

Kornburger, Michael and Jeremy Dobos. Private Military Companies: *Analyzing the Use of Armed Contractors*. Master's thesis. Naval Postgraduate School, 2007.

Krahmann, Elkhe. S*tates, Citizens, and the Privatization of Security*. New York: Cambridge University Press, 2010.

Leander, Anna. *Eroding State Authority? Private Military Companies and the Legitimate Use of Force*. Rome: Rubbettino Editore, 2006.

Meyerson, Michael I. *Liberty's Blueprint: How Madison and Hamilton Wrote the Federalist Papers, Defined the Constitution, and Made Democracy Safe for the World*. New York: Basic Books, 2008.

Military Extraterritorial Jurisdiction Act of 2000, 18 U.S.C. §§ 3261–67 (2006).

Office of Management and Budget (OMB). Executive Office of the President. OMB Circular. No. A–76. Revised. 2003.

Pincus, Walter. Increase in Contracting Intelligence Jobs Raising Concerns. *Washington Post*, March 20, 2006.

Project on National Security Reform (PNSR). *Forging a New Shield: Executive Summary.* Washington, DC: Author, November, 2008.

Ratner, Steven R. Corporations and Human Rights: A Theory of Legal Responsibility. *Yale Law Journal* 111 (2001): 490–498.

Report of the Commision on Army Acquisition and Program Management in Expeditionary Operations (Gansler Commission). October 31, 2007; available at www.army.mil/docs/gansler_commssion_report_final_071031.pdf.

Rosen, Stephen P. "Vietnam and the American Theory of Limited War," *International Security* 7 (1982): 80–85.

Saifur, Rahman. "Call to Take Advantage of Opportunities in Iraq," *Gulf News* (Dubai, United Arab Emirates). April 21, 2004.

Scahill, Jeremy. *Blackwater, The Rise of the World's Most Powerful Mercenary Army.* New York: Nation Books, 2007.

Schwartz, Moshe. Congressional Research Service. R 40764. Department of Defense Contractors in Iraq and Afghanistan: Background and Analysis 5. (2010).

Singer, P.W. *Corporate Warriors. The Rise of the Privatized Military Industry.* Ithaca, NY: Cornell University Press, 2003.

———. War, Profits, and the Vacuum of Law: Privatized Military Firms and International Law. *Columbia Journal of Transnational Law* 42 no. 521. (2004): 545–46.

Spearin, Christopher. *Privatized Peace? Assessing the interplay between states, humanitarians and private security companies.* New York: Routledge Press, 2008.

Special Maritime and Territorial Jurisdiction Statute, 18 U.S.C. § 7 (2006).

Special Inspector General, Iraq Reconstruction (SIGIR). *Quarterly Report to the United States Congress.* SIGIR, July 2011.

Status of Forces Agreement (SOFA) between Iraq and the United States, http://greatpowerpolitics.com/?tag=sofa, accessed 12 May 2011.

Szayna, Thomas S., Kevin F. McCarthy, Jerry M. Sollinger, Linda J. Demaine, Jefferson P. Marquis, and Brett Steele. "The Civil–Military Gap in the United States: Does It Exist, Why, and Does It Matter?" No. MG–379–A. Santa Monica, CA: RAND Corporation. 2007, xvi–xvii.

Stanger, Allison. *One Nation Under Contract: The Outsourcing of American Power and the Future of Foreign Policy.* New Haven, CT: Yale University Press, 2009.

Texas Tech University. "Investigation of US Economic and Military Assistance Program in Vietnam." 12 October, 1966. Online library resources accessed at http://www.virtual.vietnam.ttu.edu.

Uniform Code of Military Justice, 10 U.S.C. §§ 801–946 (2006).

United States Government Accounting Office. Considerable documentation provided from 2007–2011 on OIF expenditures and interests. Accessed at http://www.gao.gov/. Specific historical documents listed below.

————. 2003. *Military Operations: Contractors Provide Vital Services to Deployed Forces but Are Not Adequately Addressed in DoD Plans.* GAO-03-695. Washington, D.C.: GAO. http://www.gao.gov/new.items/d03695.pdf .

————. 2003. *Sourcing and Acquisition: Challenges Facing the Department of Defense.* GAO-03-574T. Washington, D.C.: GAO. http://www.gao.gov/new.items/d03574t.pdf.

————. 2004. *Contract Management: Contracting for Iraq Reconstruction and for Global Logistics Support.* GAO-04-869T. Washington, D.C.: GAO.

————. 2004. *Rebuilding Iraq: Fiscal Year 2003 Contract Award Procedures and Management Challenges.* GAO-04-605. Washington, D.C.: GAO. http://www.gao.gov/new.items/d04605.pdf .

————. 2005. *Contract Management: Opportunities to Improve Surveillance on Department of Defense Contracts.* GAO-05-274. Washington, D.C.: GAO. http://www.gao.gov/new.items/d05274.pdf.

————. 2005. *Rebuilding Iraq: Actions Needed to Improve Use of Private Security Providers.* GAO-05-737. Washington, D.C.: GAO. http://www.gao.gov/highlights/d05737high.pdf .

————. 2006. *Contract Management: DoD Vulnerabilities to Contracting Fraud, Waste, and Abuse.* GAO-06-838R. Washington, D.C. GAO. http://www.gao.gov/new.items/d06838r.pdf.

————. 2006. *Iraq Contract Costs: DoD Consideration of Defense Contracting Audit Agency's Findings.* GAO-06-1132. Washington, D.C.: GAO. http://www.gao.gov/new.items/d061132.pdf.

United States Library of Congress. *2004. Private Security Contractors in Iraq: Background, Legal Status, and Other Issues.* by Jennifer Elsea and Nina Serafino. CRS Order Code RL32419. Accessed at http://www.opencrs.com/rpts/RL32419_20040528.pdf .

United States National Security Strategy, Office of the President of the United States. 2010. Available at www.whitehouse.gov/docs/nss.

U.S. Senate, Committee on Armed Services, HRG. 111–571, *Contracting in a Counterinsurgency: An Examination of the Blackwater Paravant Contract and the Need for Oversight*, Hearing Before the Committee on Armed Services, United States Senate. One Hundred Eleventh Congress. Second Session. February 24. 2010.

Voluntary Principles on Security and Human Rights. Accessed at http://www.voluntaryprinciples. org/principles/introduction.

Weber, Max. *Economy and Society: An Outline of Interpretive Sociology*. Edited by Gunther Roth and Claus Wittich. Berkeley: University of California Press, 1978.

_____. *Essays in Sociology*. New York: Oxford University Press, 1946.

Yasin, Huma, Playing Catchup: *Proposing the Creation of Status-Based Regulations to Bring Private Military Contractor Firms Within the Purview of International and Domestic Law*. Professionl Report written as a L.L.M. Candidate, Southern Methodist University School of Law. 2012.

Zamparelli, Steven J. "Competitive Sourcing and Privatization. Contractors on the Battlefield: What Have We Signed Up For?" *Air Force Journal of Logistics* 23 no. 3 (1999): 7–14.

www.ingramcontent.com/pod-product-compliance
Lightning Source LLC
Chambersburg PA
CBHW081836280526
45789CB00007B/2471